TECHNIQUES AND EXERCISES

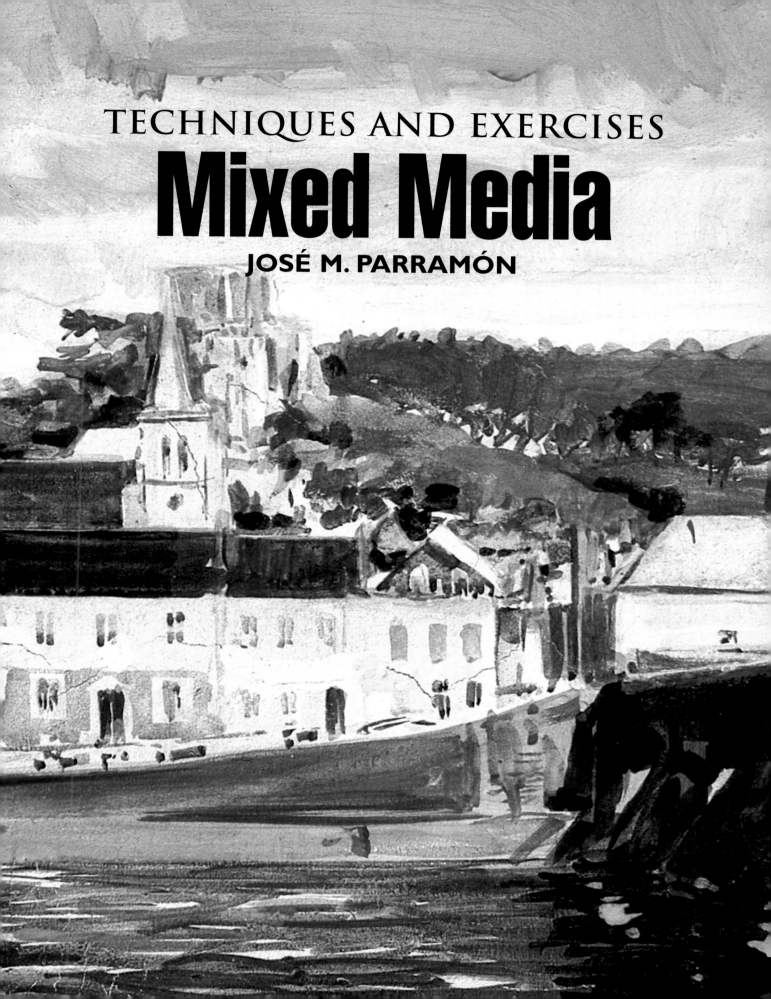

TECHNIQUES AND EXERCISES
Mixed Media
JOSÉ M. PARRAMÓN

The guides at the end of the book are numbered in the margin and have been designed to be cut with a paper cutter.

Director: José M. Parramón
Text: José M. Parramón and Gabriel Martín
Edition, layout and proofs: Ediciones Lema, S.L.
Front cover: Award
Editorial Director: José M Parramón
Editor: Victoria Sánchez
Coordination : Eduard Hernández
Translated from the Spanish by Monica Krüger

Photosetting: Novasis, S.A.L.

1st Edition: 1999
Copyright José M. Parramón Vilasaló
Exclusive editorial rights: Ediciones Lema, S.L.
Edited and distributed by Ediciones Lema, S.L.
Gran Via de les Corts Catalanes, 8-10, 1° 5ª A
08902 Hospitalet de Llobregat (Barcelona)

ISBN 84-89730-95-4
Printed in Spain

Index

Fig. 1. **Dublin city,** *by Gabriel Martín (private collection of the artist). The result of combining collage with acrylics and oils is dramatic. An amalgam of brilliant colors contrasts with patches of muted colors.*

Fig. 2. **Sunset,** *by Bibiana Crespo (private collection of the artist). This work is two meters high, the artist often uses canvases of this size as they give her freedom to work with more fluidity. This work is painted in latex paint, with finishing touches in oil.*

Fig. 3. **Pettigo,** *by Gabriel Martín (private collection of the artist). The mixed media technique allows for a freedom of style, a mixture of materials and creative processes combined in the same work.*

Introduction

The technical aspects of painting have evolved considerably across the centuries, we now have an overwhelming diversity of media at our fingertips. Before such a range of choices was available to artists, they had to have an understanding of how each of these media would respond to working with certain techniques. A knowledge of the materials and how to handle them; their composition and mixing methods, was crucial. Knowledge and mastery were the fundamental starting points for any artist.

The German artist Emil Nolde wrote about how an understanding of the technical aspect of painting is invaluable: "Painting is the art of representing a simple concept in two dimensions... The painter is interpreting his personal experiences, transforming them into a work of art. Learning to use the most suitable media is a continual exercise, there are no fixed rules. The rules are created in tandem with the creation of each work and they are dependant on the personality of their creator, his technique and his aims... The elevation of the subject stems from the fact that it has been transformed by the impulse of the artist to capture it on canvas".

However, it would seem that many of the artist's manuals forget being overly concerned with history and subject to focus on the knowledge of artists' materials and how they are to be used, it is not enough to have an artistic eye, the artist also needs the skills to express his interpretation of the subject in the right medium. Artists of the past had a sound understanding of pigments and other materials that they worked with because they made up the colors themselves, something that very rarely happens nowadays. Thanks to modern technology, ready prepared colors are now mass produced; technical advances ensure significant improvements in quality and prepared colors are readily available from any art shop. However, the craftsmanship of the artist-artisan must be learned, by returning to the roots. When you understand how to work with the base materials, see how easy it is to paint following the same simple principles and methods that were used to create history's most famous masterpieces by the Great Masters.

This book presents the reader with all the knowledge they need in order to master the mixed media techniques used today by focusing on the range of media and materials available. Works of art are examined through study of their medium, the painting process and the tools used. This explains the creative processes inherant in a two dimensional piece of art (there are cases where materials create three dimensional art, for instance using impasto or overlaying materials on the canvas, but the final result is pictorial not sculptural.) "The laws concerning artists' materials stand firm for all artists whomsoever they may be, whatever their vocation, whatever their nature."

However, all this knowledge is to little effect if you do not work; do not paint or use your skills. To that purpose this book contains exercises with guidelines so that you can experiment and reproduce the step by step demonstrations given by various skilled artists. As you will see, the methods and materials used in each of the exercises vary greatly, in such a way that the pictorial process is lent a more creative and exploratory dimension, something that is not always to be found in other art books on the market.

Evidently, the theme of materials and their uses is a popular subject amongst artists, but each has his own view. Through practice, you will see what a liberating effect mixed media has on your work: you will be freed from academic rules. You will see how unrestrictive and mind-expanding these techniques are, not only will they give you experience working with different media and creating new textures and effects, you will also go on to question the way you perceive the subject. Learning to look at your subject matter in a new light, using your imagination, reinterpreting a model in whom you see potential and even painting subjects that do not exist outside of your imagination. Leonardo da Vinci, in his Treatise on Painting, wrote a few lines of advice to the artist about how to arouse and develop their inventiveness : " (it is very useful to) look at walls mottled with colored patches or at stones made up of different colors. If you have to imagine a place you will find a similar diversity of landscape right there. A varied scene of mountains, rivers, rocks, trees, great planes, valleys and hills of various shapes appears, and there you can see battles and strange figures moving about hurriedly and an infinity of things which can be reduced to the essence; all this is evident when you look at these mottled walls just as in the tolling of bells you can make out any word or name that you care to imagine."

That said, all that is left for me to do is encourage you to get to work. I leave you with your studies, hoping that you will become fascinated by these materials and mixed media techniques.

Gabriel Martín

Fig.4. *Fields* by Emil Nolde (Lothar-Günter collection, Buchheim). Admire the use of impasto and layers of paint. This medium allows the artist to experiment, creating dramatic effects and textures. However, the use of bold blocks of colour prohibits the definition of details in the work.

MATERIALS AND ARTISTIC PROCEDURES

Developing a work of mixed media i.e. using two or more distinct paint mediums combined in a single picture, requires an understanding of the different materials that we are going to employ. The changes that pigments undergo when binding agents are introduced and the effect of mixing different techniques within the same work are observations that need to be studied. The following chapters attempt to introduce the reader to the complex but exciting world of mixed media. We will start with the basics; materials and their components, and conclude with examples of a number of new effects and textures which you can soon begin to incorporate into your work. You will then come to appreciate how valuable this knowledge is in order to master the use of mixed media in your work.

Artists and Artisans

During the Middle Ages, when the skills of craftsmanship among artists were far more evident than they are today, the division of labor was far more closely defined dependant on the particular skill of each artist. There were goldsmiths, carpenters, dyers, engravers, painters, ceramicists, bronze workers etc.

During this time, the artist would progress, from the assistant of the medieval guild workshop, through a training where he learned the fundamentals of his trade which would give him the opportunity to climb the ladder to art schools and academies. It was due to the arrival of the Renaissance that the division was made between artisan and artist, a rift developed between manual work and intellect. It was from this time that art became considered a lofty science, worthy of listing amongst the classical disciplines (philosophy, theology, architecture..), so

art, science and technology became a supreme Trinity. The Arts spanned from the plastic arts to literature, their emphasis was on the intellect of the creators, artists were considered on a par with humanists. Alberti, in his writings on architecture had already differentiated between the three main disciplines of the Arts: architecture, sculpture and painting. These were considered the high arts while other arts such as engraving, drawing, ceramics or watercolor were considered lesser arts.

Fig.5. In this illustration, which represents an iron worker's trade, the character appears surrounded by the tools of his trade. Publication by William Caxton (The Chess Game, 1483)

Fig.6. Louis XIV of France visiting the studio of the Gobelin family of dyers. Working as an assistant in a workshop was fundamentally important in this era if you wanted to learn the trade.

Despite this apparent triumph of intellectual over manual work, the Renaissance artist had to undergo training and study techniques in the studios of the great masters. They went to them to learn the trade; preparation of colors, the rules of perspective, theories of composition and the treatment and priming of canvases. In his Libro del arte, Cennino Cennini writes about what he had to study as a young artist in the fourteenth century:

"One has to join the studio of a master who has a knowledge of all the skills inherent in our craft, to grind down colors, to learn to prepare glue and plaster, to practice priming the boards, embossing and sanding down; gold leaf and the preparation of stone surfaces over a period of six years. Then one should practice the techniques of applying colors and mordants, mastering the use gold under flesh tints, learning to work on murals, all during the next six years, continually studying, never ceasing for a moment, day in and day out. In this way, while getting familiarised with these processes one gains a sound training".

So, his explanation shows us how apprentices were trained in the crafts required by an artist.

Artists have to acquire a range of skills to practice their craft, they must learn to use their materials. The best learning method is to start by mixing your own colors and preparations just the way they did in the Middle Ages, starting with powdered pigments and binding agents. To work through each of these processes in this way gives you the optimum understanding of the composition of different substances and enables you to see how they react to various mixing methods. Becoming aquainted with the materials, understanding the rationale of their application, and practical use of them, leads to the mastery of the techniques of mixed media.

7

Fig.7. The apprentice of the studio would have to start by learning how to prepare colors and to prime the canvases so that their masters could begin their work.

Fig.8. **The artist's studio** *(Musée du Louvre, Paris)* **by Gustave Courbet. The** *artist represents himself in the centre of the scene, he appears to be adding the final touches to one of his works. At his back, a number of contemporary intellectuals are gathered, they represent his brotherhood in the arts; literature, philosophy, and music.*

8

Dividing the Disiplines of Art

As we have already mentioned, it was Alberti who made the distinction between the major disciplines of the arts: architecture, sculpture and painting. It has been the distinction of these three "high arts" that the schools of art based their studies on and today's academies and schools follow in their footsteps but with one failing, today's arts faculties have converted themselves into centers of theoretical study and have dismissed the technical crafts of the arts.

Fortunately, the fundamental questions of art still cannot be answered without taking the basic building blocks into account. Answering these questions requires an understanding of media, canvases and procedures, especially those that have developed more recently from the 1950's. So, in addition to the traditional artists' crafts, one also needs an understanding of newer developments such as the use of mixed media.

This new combination of materials and techniques in a work confounds the distinctions between the traditional disciplines. So, should collage of three dimensional objects on canvas or low relief works produced with crushed marble be considered painting or sculpture? It is evident that the traditional divisions of the "high arts" drawn up by Alberti are losing their meaning in today's world. Today, the crafts associated with art, particularly technical skills, should be considered according to their production system; their choice of support, materials and procedures. One has to bear in mind that these techniques and materials have developed to make mixed media possible. Many contemporary artworks cannot be classified into categories such as watercolors, oils, pastels or etchings.

9

Figs.9, 10, 11. Images of the three major artistic disciplines as defined by Alberti. The church of the Consolation in Todi is an example of the symmetry which dominated religious architecture of the Renaissance (fig.9).

10

11

This focus on symmetry is also evident in sculptural groups such as La Pieta by Michealangelo (St. Peter's, Rome) (fig.10). The same symmetry is evident in painting as well as sculpture, the pyramidal format was the most popular, particularly when representing holy figures such as this Madonna del jilguero by Rafael (Uffizi, Florence) (fig.11).

The majority of these works are painted using a mixture of media and styles and, although they may use unusual materials and techniques, that doesn't make them any less significant than any other composition created using more traditional methods.

The methods used to develop a mixed media work are not considered an end in themselves, they are merely a starting point in the long process of exploration that the artist embarks on in his work. However, one must bear in mind that the artist's creativity is paramount and he must have the curiosity to attempt new combinations, compositions and textures; if not he runs the risk of seeing himself cast as a mere technician, hopelessly restricted by his medium.

Fig.12. Rafael's vision represented in his work **The Academy of Athens** *(Vatican chambers) is fairly typical of the role that art played during the Renaissance; art more closely affiliated to philosophy and literature than to the workshop of the craftsman. It is the conceptual idea rather than the skill of the craftsman that is most important in this case.*

The Earliest Mixed Media Works

13

Mixed media is best defined as the use of different media in the same work or a combination of surfaces to paint on such as newspaper, wood or cardboard. It is obvious that the choice of materials is of great importance in the creative process.

Mixed media work requires a variety of different procedures. These pictorial procedures can vary greatly and they depend on the binding agent used in combination with the color pigments.

According to Max Doerners account in his book "The materials of painting", it is possible that one of the first artists to tackle works in mixed media was Jan Van Eyck, "It is highly likely that the breakthrough was made not through the discovery of a completely unknown new substance but through the chance combination and application of substances that were already at hand".

Van Eyck applied a base coat of tempera and finished the work with touches of oil. The rapid drying of the tempera worked well with the beautiful varnish finish which covered the layers of oil. The water based tempera paints make highly detailed work possible, the colors stand out more dramatically. The use of oils lend the work more clarity of detail. "I would add to this that the tempera doesn't dissolve when the oil paint is added."

14

Figs 13 & 14. Despite the growth in popularity that mixed media techniques have enjoyed during the twentieth century, these techniques stem from long ago. In the fifteenth century Jan van Eyck was already experimenting with a combination of media in his work; see the two examples: **The Madonna of Chancellor Rolin** *(Musée du Louvre, Paris, fig.13) and* **The Madonna with Cannon van de Paele** *(Groeningemuseum, Bruges, fig.14), both painted using a combination of tempera and oil.*

At this point it would be useful to summarize the two basic rules of mixed media, first, you must know how to select your media and bring out the best of each medium that you use, so that you choose the ideal media for the result you are looking to achieve. (it is evident that the richness and brilliance of the finish in Van Eyck's paintings can only be achieved through the use of a thick medium such as oil). Second, you need to find the most compatible combination of media, in order to avoid the running of colors, unsatisfactory fixing, and combinations of different media that "clash" on the same canvas. So, by considering these issues, a mixed media work will prove a success, the expressive qualities of the work are evoked through use of a combination of different materials and techniques.

Figs.15, 16 & 17. Oil and acrylic are the two media that are most commonly seen used together in one work. This combination is currently very popular. Here are three examples of works painted by contemporary artists: **Enninskillen** *by Gabriel Martín (private collection of the artist) (fig.15);* **Still Life with fruit** *by Bibiana Crespo (private collection of the artist) (fig.16) and* **Nude by a lamp** *(private collection of the artist) (fig.17).*

Pigments and other Colorants

Pigments are dry solids often found in a powdered form which can be combined with a variety of binding agents, the resulting substances are used as the basis of all known painting media. Specialist shops sell an impressive range of pigments. If you want to experiment with a range of different media you may be better off buying a small selection of powdered pigments. Once you have the colors and you decide what medium you want to work in, all you need do is mix the pigment with the right binding agent. This way you won't have to waste money on buying an endless number of tubes of color for each different technique.

Colorants fall into two categories; organic and inorganic. There are four subclassifications within these main groups:

Inert pigments: These are the least affected by light and the most durable. They are made from the oxides of iron, aluminum, manganese and cobalt (Ochre, Sienna, Van Dyke Brown, Mars Black, Red Lead, Manganese Green, Blue Manganese, Cobalt Blue, Red Cobalt and Emerald Green amongst others).

Sulphates: Include cadmium sulphate, zinc sulphate and highly luminescent colors (Cadmium Yellow, Zinc White, a range of orange colors...).

Lead and copper based pigments: Highly reactive to light (Lead White, Chrome Yellow, Veronese Green, Copper Blue, Venetian Brown, etc.).
Sensative pigments: Pigments such as Prussian Blue, Cinnabar Green, English Green and Vermilion all blacken when in contact with air.

Fig.18. Once mixed with the binding agent, the pigments are the basis of all pictorial techniques.

18

On the other hand, there is another group of colors of both organic and synthetic origin which differ from the mineral extracts just discussed (aniline, alizarin, scarlet, cyan, squid ink etc.). The strength of color of each pigment varies dependant on the size of the particles. This is logical, if you weigh a certain quantity of a pigment, the smaller the size of the particles, the greater the combined surface area. This explains why Ivory Black and Titanium White have a more saturated color than Mars Black and Zinc White.

I suggest you try a simple experiment if you want to compare the color strength of pigments: take two measures of Ultramarine Blue (e.g. coffee spoonfuls in two separate piles). Just place the piles side by side on a piece of glass and add an equal measure of Titanium White to one, and Zinc White to the other. If you add linseed oil and mix the colors with a spatula, you will observe a marked difference in depth of color in the two mixtures. This serves as an illustration of the different effects of the two types of white pigment.

From this experiment we can deduct that no two pigments will behave in the

Fig 19. Each pigment has a different saturation strength. Here, the same mix of Ultramarine blue is treated with Zinc White (left) and Titanium White (right) and it is clear that Titanium White is a far more saturated color.
Fig.20. Today, squid ink can be bought in powdered form, it is sold in bags weighing half a kilo.
Fig.21. Just add a bit of water to the powdered squid ink to obtain a rich dark liquid.

19
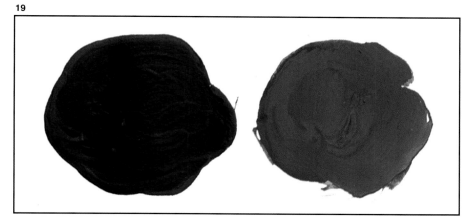

20

21

same way, and that many of them also differ in their ability to cover the base onto which they are applied; the quantity of binding agent needed in order to obtain the correct paste-like consistency; in the soundness and stability of the paint obtained, i.e. the amount the paint's tone alters once it is dry on the canvas; and the variation of color over a period of time, as air and light act as catalysts in the alteration of the paint's chemical formula.

It is impossible to calculate the number of different pigments that are manufactured. If you want to buy pigments I have listed a number that will make up a basic color palette. You only need 10 colors: Raw Sienna, Burnt Umber, Yellow Ochre, Titanium White, Ultramarine Blue, Prussian Blue, Emerald Green, Cadmium Yellow, Red Carmine and Ivory Black.

Raw Sienna: Originated from Sienna, although it was subsequently used throughout Tuscany and Sardinia. It contains a considerable quantity of iron hydrates, which give it the characteristic red color. Of all the colors selected here it is the most difficult to prepare, it requires a great quantity of binding agent.

Burnt Umber: Umber pigments are obtained by grinding rocks containing managese and iron and they vary in tone from ochre to a deep brown. This is the most versatile pigment used in all paint media and it is compatible with all other pigments.

Yellow Ochre: Originates from the decomposition of the minerals iron and feldspar. It covers well and is highly saturated. It is lightfast and stable in water but sensitive to acids.

Titanium White: I recommend this white because of all white pigments it has the best covering power and is highly saturated. It is also resilient, and lasts well over time staying true to its original color. It is suitable for all media.

Ultramarine Blue: This color was manufactured to provide an alternative to the highly expensive and rare lapis lazuli used in the Middle Ages.

It is one of the hardest pigments to mix with water, I recommend that you add a little ethylene alcohol to the mixture. Also bear in mind that it is not ideal for work exposed outdoors or in badly ventilated or damp rooms as the humidity will affect the color.

Prussian Blue: Also known as Paris Blue it is a pigment containing iron. It is labelled as "water soluble" and very popular in watercolor painting, however it is not so easy to work with in oil media.

Emerald Green: A highly resilient pigment, with excellent covering power and a long drying time. The most stable green pigment available, it is ideal for any medium, including fresco or casein which may be used outdoors.

Cadmium Yellow: Composed of crys-

22a

tals of cadmium sulphur, this pigment has excellent covering power. One factor to bear in mind: given the high sensitivity of this pigment to acids, it can only be used for indoor painting, it cannot be exposed to the elements.

Red Carmine: This pigment is found in cochineal beetles which live in a certain family of cactus plants. The depth and beauty of this color exceeds any other, however, it is not entirely light resistant.

Ivory Black: This is the most well known black pigment. It is made from carbonised bone (originally made by heating ivory), it is also known as Bone Black. The phosphate particles it contains give it a slightly greyish blue tint.

This selection has been made choosing colors considered indispensable to the artist. That said, the painter has to choose -- if he is to buy his own pigments -- dependant on the use to which he is going to put the colors rather than the tones of the colors.

Figs.22a, 22b, 22c. There is a huge variety of color pigments on the market. As you would do with any kind of paint, you should start working with the basic pigments, a small selection comprising of indispensable colors.

22c

Binding agents and Solvents

Binding agents are substances in a liquid form, which, when combined with pigment will harden and stick the paint to the surface of the canvas. Once the mixture is made, the particles of the pigment are bound together in suspension in the binding medium. They can then easily be applied to the surface to be painted.

The artist should have a variety of binding agents at hand in order to make up paints for the most popular paint media. The choice of binding agent is dependant on the consistency, viscosity and drying time, the adherence and the covering power and resistance to the elements desired of the resulting medium. I have listed a selection of the most common binding agents: refined linseed oil, acrylic binder, gum arabic, casein and egg.

Linseed oil: An oil extracted from the seeds of flax which can be used both as a binding medium and as a thinner for oil painting.

Synthetic medium: A solution for binding and diluting made synthetically. It is an emulsion of extremely fine resin particles. If this is mixed with pigment, acrylic is produced. It is also called artificial resin.

Gum Arabic: A vegetable extract deriving from acacia resin. The most common binding agent for watercolor, gouache and similar media.

Latex: A synthetic product with a milky appearance, similar in consistency to the sap of the rubber tree (from the acacia family). It is one of the most effective media for securing paint to a support.

Casein: A phosphorproteinous binding agent made up of milk proteins. It is often associated with tempera painting.

Egg: The mixture of egg yolk with pigment and distilled water combines to make egg tempera. This binding agent creates a coat of hard durable paint. Some artists have used egg yolk as a highly effective varnish finish.

Binding agents play a vital role in pictorial techniques, the qualities of the resulting different paints determine which is chosen and the technique used in the picture (gouache, watercolor, oil, tempera, acrylic etc.).

Fig.23.Sometimes binding agents are available in a solid state.They come from natural glues,gums and oils which,when mixed with water or turps become an ideal agent to mix with the pigment.

23

Some substances can act both as thinners and binding agents. In oil and acrylic paintings the same substance is used as both thinner and binding agent, the solvent is different. On the other hand, in watercolor painting the binding agent is gum, while the solvent and the thinner is water.

By solvents we are referring to liquids that dissolve the paints. They can be used to obtain a particular consistency or to prevent the paint drying until the task is finished. You can divide media into two categories, those with a gum or resin binding agent can be diluted with water, while those which have oily binding agents need quick evaporating solvents which won't alter the characteristics of the paint. Here is a list of the most common solvents.

Water: The most widely used solvent; generally used with paint containing gum as its principal binding agent.

Ethyl alcohol: A powerful solvent for resin, it is also used to help dissolve powdered pigment in water or so that it binds better with the binding agent.

Turpentine: Be sure that this is distilled, the turpentine that is generally sold in shops has a tendency to yellow the paint. As well as being one of the most efficient solvents of oil paints it is also the solvent that gives off the most fumes. Constant exposure to turps causes skin irritation.

White spirits: A volatile substance derived from petroleum which evaporates very quickly. Solvents which evaporate at such speed are dangerous to your health so always work in well ventilated areas.

Sansodor: A solvent which evaporates as quickly as turps but it doesn't give off such bad fumes and is not as bad for your health. For this reason it is a good alternative to the other solvents.

Fig.24. Solvents always come in a liquid form and are used to dissolve the paint off the paintbrush as well as for thinning paint.

24

Mixed Media

Painting techniques can be divided into two main groups:

a) Water based techniques: the group of paints that make up substances that are water soluble (gum, wax and silicates);

b) Oil based techniques: all paints that need an oily binding agent (natural or artificial).

It is best to start by only mixing media which belong to the same group, but as we will see later, there are some exceptions worth mentioning. We will go over the different media and look at which are compatible and which are not. Given that pastel consists of a pigment in powder form compounded with gesso and bound with gum arabic and that it is usually applied dry, this medium can be combined with watercolor, tempera or with gouache, as it is of the same group. Pastel is very different from watercolor which requires a considerable amount of water so that the paint is spread thinly over the surface of the paper leaving a soft, transparent layer of color, so that the white support shows through. Watercolors can also be mixed or diluted with gum arabic, this creates a paint similar to tempera, mixing this medium with egg tempera or gouache works well. Tempera and gouache differ from watercolor in that they are not transparent, but opaque and paste-like, this makes these media very useful to add finishing touches to watercolor and when painting outdo-

ors. While gouache works well when applied to paper, tempera can be applied to any support. As we have already discussed, tempera, with its egg binding agent, has been used in combination with Oil paints since the Middle Ages.

This is one of the few water based media which can be mixed with an oil based medium, this combination has traditionally been the most popular mixed media technique.

Fig.25. Oil paints are the best known of all oil based media. They are called oil paints as their main binding agent is linseed oil.

25

26

27

Fig.26. Pastels can be diluted with water as they are basically made up of powdered pigment. However, they don't contain a binding agent, their hold on the support is minimal, Pastels are fragile and easily worn off.

Fig.27. Water based techniques are distinguished from oil based by their gum based binding agents which are water soluble. The most popular are watercolor, gouache and acrylic.

This is not the only exception however, more recently developed plastic and latex based media can also be used in combination with oil paint. Just bear this in mind though: tempera and acrylic tend to be used as base coats, i.e. the oil is always added over the top once the base has dried; it has to be this way round. Tempera and acrylic do not have the adhesive power to be painted over oil paint.

The mixture of pigment with oil is the basis of all oil based painting, oils can be used on any support, although they are particularly suitable for specially prepared fabric or canvas.

Oil is a perfect medium for creating texture and impasto, it is also works well in combination with encaustic painting (painting with wax) or with powdered minerals such as crushed marble or silicon carbide.

Encaustic painting requires the artist to work with hot wax, it can be used in combination with the oil paint on the same support. When working with powdered minerals however, they are applied first in a paste form, having been mixed with latex glue. Once this preparation is dry the oil paints are layered on top.

And lastly, to finish off this chapter, a word about lacquer. As a solid it comes in the form of flakes and is only soluble in alcohol. Sometimes it may be necessary to mix in some powdered pumice stone, the result being that when applied it shines like crystal. While lacquer is often used to decorate a wide range of objects, it's not unusual for it to be mixed with alcohol aniline or used to add finishing touches to an oil painting.

28

*Fig.28. **Nude** by Bibiana Crespo (private collection of the artist). The two media used here are oil and acrylic, probably one of the most popular mixed media techniques.*
*Fig.29. **The Bridge** by Preston Dickinson (The Newark Museum; Purchase) an example of a combination of media in the same work: pastel, gouache and pencil on paper.*

29

Useful Equipment

As well as the support, traditional paintbrushes etc., there are a whole host of other materials that are necessary for the preparation and creation of a mixed media work. The pieces of equipment which are described here

30

are easy to get hold of and inexpensive.

A. Hotplate: This is something you should always have on hand as many of the preparations have to be heated (casein, encaustic, rabbit skin glue).

B. Pans: It is useful if possible to have

a selection of pans of different sizes which will fit inside one another, as the majority of the mixtures must be prepared using a double boiler.

C. Empty containers: Plastic or glass containers for storing a preparation

once it has been made.

D. Receptacles for thinners: these should be fairly large as water and turps dirty very quickly and this could spoil the colors. Some artists use two containers, one to wash brushes and the other to use for mixing with colors.

E. A wooden board: The board can be used as a backing support to paint on, fix the paper on to it with sticky tape, leave a white margin all around the paper so it can be unstuck easily when the painting is finished. The board is useful whether working in the studio or in the open air.

When outdoors, work on small scale paintings, it's best to use an easel (they come in various guises from a simple aluminum tripods to more robust wooden models).

F. Paper clips: are used to hold the paper to the board. The best are bull-dog clips which are the widest.

G. Bowls: These are for mixing paints and can be ceramic or any other resistant material.

H. Spatula: Used to prepare large quantities of paint and to prevent wastage. When painting on a larger canvas it can also be used as a scraper.

I. Alcohol: as well as speeding up the drying process of oil paint it is also used to facilitate the mixing of pigment with the binding agent.

J. Sponges: These can be natural or synthetic. They are usually used to create different textures on the surface of the paper.

Objets Trouvés

What with the voracity of today's consumer and the importance of recycling, the artist finds himself in a favorable position. All the leftovers produced by our neighbours offer us a host of artistic possibilities, just one example of how modern life can benefit the artist.

These objets trouvés hardly ever cost anything and they can be the source of work as interesting as any picture created using more traditional methods. Don't simply select random objects, consider the pictorial possibilities of each object before you choose it.

This is no easy task, it requires considerable imagination, versatility and judgement. The objects should be a springboard for the development and expression of your ideas, a new media for experimenting with alternative compositions. This process requires far more consideration than the exercise of merely sitting down to paint in front of a model.

Look at the examples here of how objets trouvés are used by the German dadaist artist, Kurt Schwitters. These works are created through the use of collage, they are made up of scraps and other leftovers that caught the artist's eye: tickets, newspaper cuttings, sweet wrappers and other bits and pieces. But he doesn't limit himself to this sort of collage, he also created works called merzbau in another media, these consisted of metallic, wooden and cardboard objects and other useless scraps.

Figs.31 & 32. Kurt Schwitters' creations are a veritable compendium of objets trouvés which, when arranged together as a collage become a cohesive composition. On this page you can see Objects in Space (detail), collage (Kunstsammlung Nordrhein Westfalen de Düsseldorf) (fig.31) and Merzbild Nº31 (Kunstsammlung Nordrhein Westfalen de Düsseldorf) (fig.32).

Two Dimensional and Flat Techniques

As a rule, water soluble paints are most suitable for painting in veils or thin washes of color, while those that are oil based can be used to create volume and texture through their use in the work.

In this way, traditional watercolor, anilines and tempera are applied in thin layers, by applying a series of washes of thin transparent paint. Each wash alters the previous color and rich, luminescent tones are created. This process is also associated with oil painting but because oil is a slow drying medium, working with lean washes requires time and patience.

However, oil painters have developed another more appropriate method which produces subtle textures using brushtrokes which merge and blend the colors.

This can be achieved painting on dry, i.e. with very little thinner. Load just a little paint onto the paintbrush and work it vigorously over the canvas. The result is a veil of color with subtle transitions between tones and delicate light and shading.

Unlike untextured painting, impasto creates volume on the surface of the picture plane, giving it an uneven, bumpy texture. This texture lends the work a more solid and expressive look and increases the impression of depth. There are a number of effective ways to achieve this impasto texture: by applying paint with a spatula, color impasto, with crushed marble, using encaustic technique or even by adding three dimensional objects as in collage...

Acrylics can also be used to give volume to paintings using these techniques. There are a variety of fast drying acrylics on the market, these can give volume to the picture's surface. Once the surface is hardened, more acrylic paint or oil paint can be added.

33

34

35

36

Figs.33 & 34. In this painting's different stages (painted by Ginés Quiñonero) you can see how the successive veils of wash have built up to form this attractive seascape. Using fine layers of color is the best method of working with watercolor.

Fig.35. Given oil's thicker consistency, it is the best medium for impasto and dense layers of color.

Fig.36. See how the impasto has been skillfully applied using oils in this beautiful flower composition by Emil Nolde (Flowers, Kunstmuseum, Düsseldorf).

Satin and Gloss

It is good to take advantage of the wide variety of different media to produce pictures that are rich and textural and to create contrasts through the presence or absence of gloss finishes. Finishes can be used to bring out and accentuate the character and the texture of a painting, with the aim of creating a deeper impression on the spectator. To achieve this, the artist often uses a coat of varnish which gives the picture's surface a sparkling uniform glaze while bringing out the depth and enriching the colors. Varnish can be applied to acrylics as well as oils (contrary to popular belief), once they have dried. Either gloss or matt varnish can be used, a mixture of the two gives a satin glaze.

The different media each have their own natural finish, matt, satin, or gloss, dependant on the composition of each medium. Many art critics will study the finish of the picture in order to identify the media used. However, it is quite common to come across mixed media works which have a variety of finishes combined in one picture. Learn to look critically at these techniques and try to use them to bring out the best in your work, don't hesitate to combine areas painted with latex paint (which has a shiny finish) with gouache (matt in appearance), this will give a greater richness to the final composition. Try combinations of media that have different qualities. Here is a short list which compares the lustre and brilliance of different media whose light reflective qualities all differ:

Media with a matt finish: watercolor, gouache, casein, aniline and fresco.

Media with a satin finish: paint containing gum arabic, acrylics, oil paint and tempera.

Media with a gloss finish: paint containing latex paint, laquers, oil painting and acrylics (if varnish is applied). It is also common to add silicon carbide to paint. This greenish grey substance which is sold in powder form is normally sprinkled on or added into the paint for a brilliant glaze.

37

38

39

40

Fig.37. Silicon carbide is sprinkled on the picture's surface to create a brilliant film, it is similar in appearance to a metallic powder.
Figs. 38, 39 & 40. Oil painting has a satin finish (Cow in a cabbage field by R. Koller, Rath Museum, Geneva, fig. 38); however, it is in medieval paintings that a perfect interplay is achieved between brilliant surfaces (gold leaf) and satin finish (tempera paint): **The Annunciation** *by Simone Martini, Uffizi, Florence (fig.39). Watercolor, by contrast, is completely matt (**In the Garden**, by August Macke, Aargamer Kunsthans, Aaran, fig.40)*

Media

As I've already discussed, it works out far cheaper if you buy the basic art materials separately; the pigments, binding agents and thinners can then be used to prepare the materials that you need when you need them.

It is fair to say that making colors at home is straightforward, it just requires careful measurement of the ingredients making up the paint, along with a good dose of patience.

In order to achieve the best results you need a marble tile, a spatula with a straight edged blade, the pigments, a mask and some latex gloves, ready prepared binding agent and empty flasks to store the concoction that you are preparing.

It's very easy. First put some pigment onto the tile, dampen it with a little water if the binding agent you are going to use is a gum derivative or a little turps if you are going to make oil paint; then mix it until all the powder is wet; add the binding agent and work the mixture until a thick paste is formed, once the mixture is made, store it in a flask made of glass or plastic. Without stabilizers or preservatives the home-made paint will only last a few months, unless they are made with rabbit skin glue or casein in which case they will deteriorate in a number of days. Anyway, don't make more paint than you envision using.

Before finishing this chapter, let me remind you of a few necessary precautions: when working with powdered pigments use a face mask and latex gloves, the high concentration of lead in pigments is bad for your health. Do not ingest anything while in contact with pigments and keep them out of the reach of children.

Fig.41. The best method of discovering how materials react when mixed is to start from the beginning. In other words, learn to make your own colors. For this you need a marble tile, binding agents, a spatula, latex gloves and a facemask and flasks to store the colors.

41

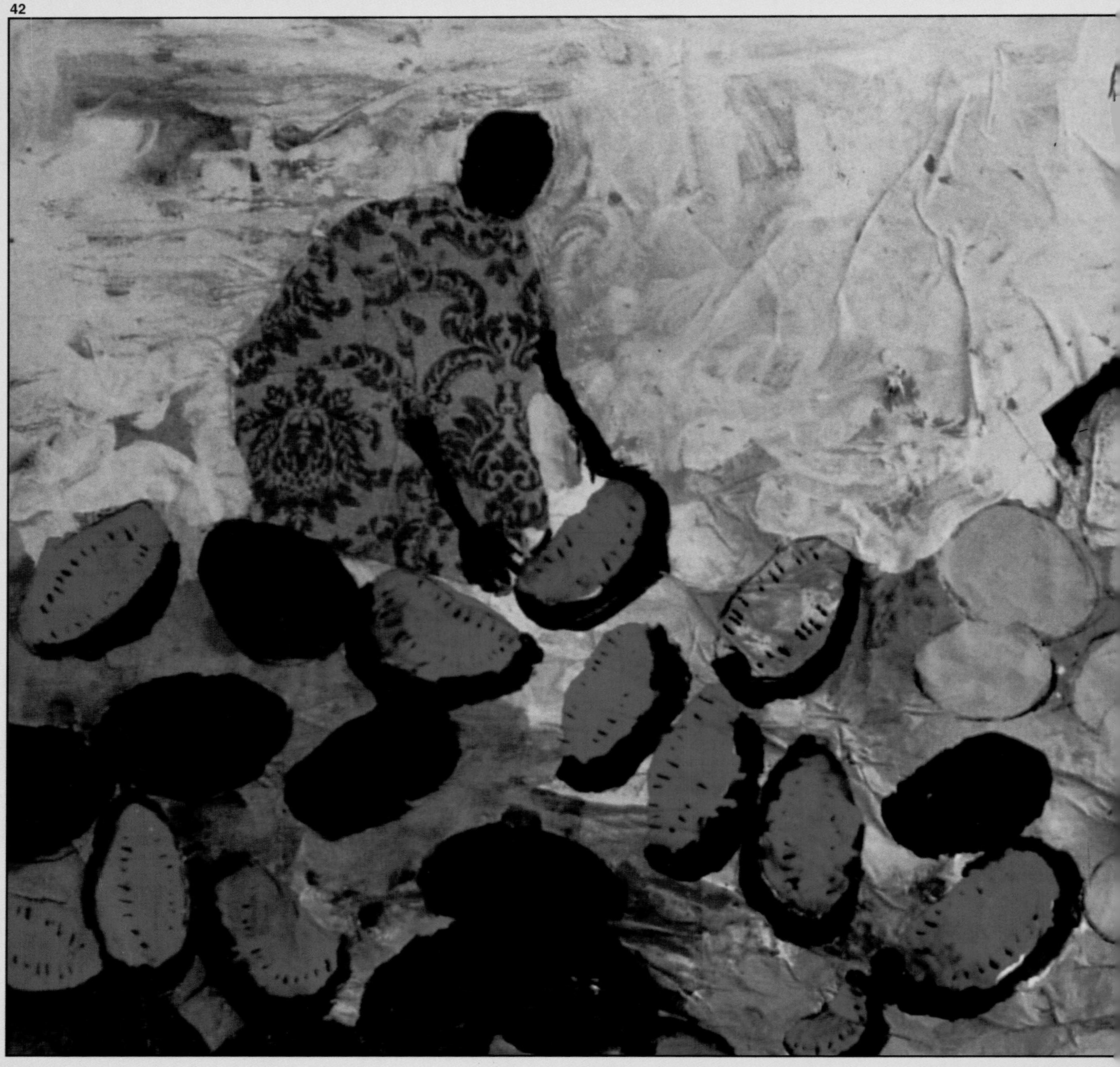

Fig.42. The combination of two different media, acrylic and paper collage, enable the artist to create spontaneous compositions with vivid colors like the one above (*In the market* by Miguel Olivares, private collection). Acrylic is an ideal medium to work with when sketching as it has such a short drying time.

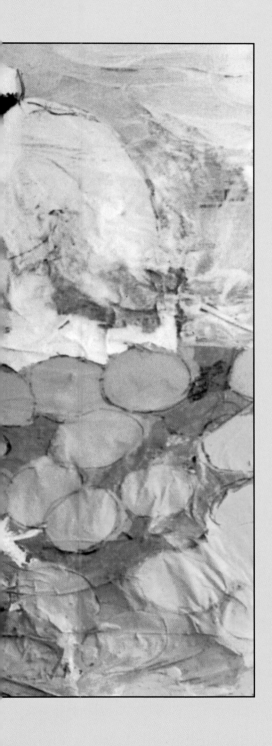

POPULAR MIXED MEDIA TECHNIQUES

The objective of the following chapters
is to introduce the most commonly used
combinations of mixed media and some
additional pictorial devices which will enable
you to further develop your individual style.
As you can see, mixed media techniques vary
greatly from one to another. They add a
further dimension to the creative process of the
artist. It is for this reason that, besides the need
to know the ingredients of each type of paint, it
is crucial to asses which are the strengths and
weaknesses of each particular medium, at each
stage of each preparation. You need to consider
these factors, forgetting these steps could result
in deterioration, cracking or flaking of the
paint from the support, which could start just
a few days after the painting is finished.

Using Collage in a Painting

Many dictionaries define collage as a process whereby cuttings or fragments of paper and a variety of other materials are stuck onto a support with the intention of creating an image or composition. Even though this process has been used since the tenth century in Japan, it was the cubists Picasso, Braque and Gris who were to transform the medium by introducing oil and watercolor into collage work.

Collage heightened the creative instincts of the artists who had started to distance themselves from traditional oil techniques which were becoming outmoded at that time. From that time, many artists who were concerned with introducing an element of chance into their work started to use mixed media and to experiment with new materials.

A profusion of work was produced by fauvists like Henri Matisse, dadaists like Kurt Schwitters and Jean Arp, and surrealists like Max Ernst.

Despite the apparent simplicity of the process, collage is a complex exercise, requiring more than simply sitting down and cutting up and pasting pieces of paper of different textures and colors. You need to learn how to see the subject in a simplified form and to summarise it in a few simple flat shapes, using a few paper cut-outs or papiers collés; pieces from newspapers, magazines or colored cards.

This technique signified the combining of different concepts and visual elements that created an effective composition. This way of working had a liberating effect, and the physical work of the composition allowed for time to reflect and interpret the way in which the subject was to be represented and to invent new ways of seeing. This approach to the subject, seen as a new philosophy of concepts and ideas, made this technique stand out from other more traditional painting methods.

Figs.43, 44 & 45. A selection of distinctive work in collage by the Spanish artist Juan Gris, we can appreciate the finesse of synthesis with which Gris composes his subjects: **Dessert dish, glass and newspaper** *(Rijksmuseum Kroller-Muller de Otterlo) (fig.43);* **Guitar** *(private collection (fig.44)* **The Blind** *(Tate gallery, London) (fig.45).*

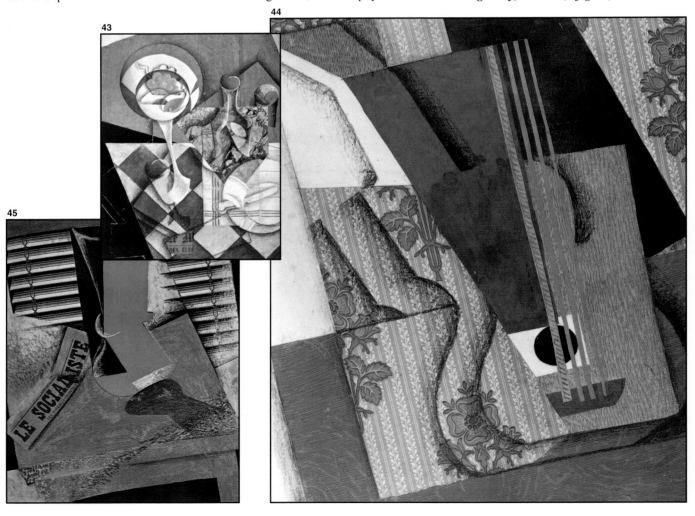

43

44

45

By experimenting with collage you will come to discover that it is possible to create a composition without slavishly imitating the objects you want to represent. Not even their true profiles or proportions are needed, this way you can experiment with the tension and interplay that develops between areas of different color as well as producing other effects more directly related to contrast and the harmonies in a range of colors. The vibrations of discordant colors are more powerful when the colors used are intense, complementary and of approximately the same tonal value. The effect of contrasts between colors is greatest on the borders where areas of strongly contrasting colors meet, in such a way that if you try to create a collage using the most strident colors you should make as many points of contact and overlap as possible between different patches of color.

That said, do not rely too heavily on this technique alone. Compositions created with collage are effective for capturing an impression or as an exercise in composition, but if you are looking to achieve a more refined, finished work I would advise that you add some touches of paint. You can combine any paint media with collage.

46

48

47

Figs.46, 47 & 48. Collage can create very visually dynamic works which use the contrast of colors or the synthesis of overlapping lines and forms. Look at **The Violin** *by Pablo Picasso (Musée National d'Art Moderne, Paris) (fig.46);* **Glasses and newspapers** *by Juan Gris (Smith College, Northampton) (fig.47), and* **The Snail** *by Henri Matisse (Tate Gallery, London) (fig 48).*

Painting in Anilines and Watercolor

Watercolors contain color pigments in powdered form. They are made up with gum arabic as a binding agent, a little tragacanth gum, a pinch of sugar and similar glues that are also water soluble. In comparison, liquid watercolors do not contain powdered pigment, they are made up of a liquid with an oily consistency which is a derivative of aniline, obtained from nitrobenzene which is used in making what we know as aniline colors. That is why this class of paints are called anilines. Both media can be used together to great effect given their different characteristics. The quality and the durability of traditional watercolor combined with the bold color and adaptability of anilines make for pleasing compositions.

The two media share many of the same properties: transparent, unopaque paints which take their luminosity from the whiteness of the paper they are applied to and are both water soluble (the more water that is added the lighter the resulting tone of color and vice versa). Once the paint is dry, the artist can make certain further alterations such as opening white spaces, scraping or adding another wash to one that is already dry. One very attractive aspect of aniline is the quality of the colors that it offers. These colors are particularly bold and saturated and they have excellent covering power. This strength of color is very useful for watercolorists when creating large dark backgrounds.

Unfortunately these colors are far less durable than traditional watercolor. In fact, given their characteristics, anilines are more closely associated with ink than with watercolor.

Watercolors are slightly grainy, which helps when creating textures and interesting effects such as opening white spaces on wet and dry, creating textures with turps and adding subsequent layers on dry, etc. If you want to open white spaces with aniline it is best to leave aside the watercolor technique and take a little bleach, adding it to the zone that you want to whiten.

You will see that after a couple of minutes

49

50

51

Fig.49. Gum arabic is the main binding agent of traditional watercolor painting, in its solid form it looks similar to amber.
Fig.50. Anilines differ from watercolors because of their composition. Their main advantage is the strength of their colors. They can be applied with a normal paintbrush or by spraying, for which you will need a toothbrush amongst your basic equipment.
Fig.51. Because they are water based, watercolors can be used with anilines or inks. This combination can be seen in Thomas Hart Benton's **Campsite** *(Allen Memorial Art Museum, Orbelin).*

the bleach has almost completely whitened the paint and a white space has been opened. Liquid watercolor works well using a spraying technique, load the paintbrush or toothbrush with a little paint, bend the bristles back with your middle finger and then let it go and the paint will spray out. This spattering technique can be used over a traditional watercolor which is already dry to add shading or texture, in the sky or in vegetation, it leaves a very fine spattering of color over the area, creating a pointillist effect. Anilines can be used to apply a series of washes, however, they are less effective because of their strength of color. When both media have been used in the same work it is preferable to apply the heavy shading and any spattering with liquid water-color, the details and volume with tradi- tional watercolors. To reiterate, using these two media together presents no problem as they both have their main characteristics in common.

Fig.52. Watercolor's advantage over aniline is its ability to cover large areas, although watercolors are not so bold as anilines. Despite the paler colors, watercolors can add a grainy texture to the work.

Fig.53. Anilines and watercolor can be combined with gouache. The background is painted with Aniline and watercolor and the gouache is used to add the details with bolder thicker colors. **Landscape mural study,** *by Stuart Davis (National Museum of American Art, Washington).*

Tempera and Gouache

Tempera and gouache differ from watercolor in that their colors are less transparent, becoming opaque when dry. This is due to the fact that they contain white gesso or Spanish white to make them thicker and more paste-like. Colours containing gesso tend to lighten as they dry as the gesso tends to have the effect of a white pigment once dry. Often these media have a similar appearance to oil although their binding agent or gum is water soluble.

Watercolor is the descendent of tempera, it contains less gum arabic and gesso and more binding agent (sometimes honey, sugar or tragacanth gum is used). However, the materials, supports and techniques used are similar in both cases.

These two media have always been linked to such an extent that many artists have used gouache to retouch or add the final touches to images created in watercolor.

This is because of the distinct ways of working with each medium. Watercolor is used with a lot of water, the pigment is applied to the surface of the paper in gentle transparent washes and the white of the paper shows through and gives brightness to the composition. White is not used in watercolor, the only white is the white of the paper. As we have already noted, tempera and gouache have excellent covering power, which enables you to superimpose colors onto the previous washes of watercolor, the same way that you would with oils. They are versatile media, the artist can chose to take advantage of this opaqueness or alternatively to create delicate subtle effects similar to watercolor.

When the two media are used in combination I suggest that you always carry out the first washes in watercolor, with this more delicate medium you can capture the subtle nuances of light and shadow and you will obtain the unique luminosity of watercolor. The fluidity and transparency of watercolor enables you to try a range of effects exploiting the whiteness of the paper which shows through. Next the colors can be strengthened, by apply-ing more intense, opaque colors. Despite the opaque qualities of gouache it is better to apply darker colors on top of lighter ones as gouache is not as opaque as oils or acrylics, the result being that some of the colors are more translucent than others.

Fig.54. **Woman putting on stockings** *by Toulouse-Lautrec (Musée Toulouse-Lautrec, Albi);* **gouache** *on card.*

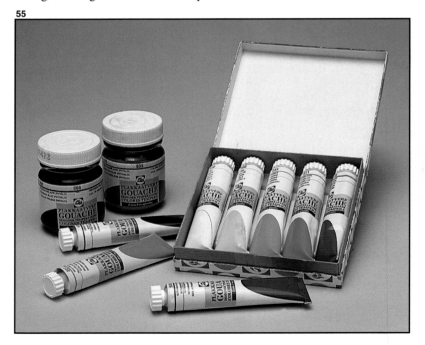

Fig.55. There are a great variety of **gouache** *products on the market. They are sold in tubes, pots and bottles often labelled "colors for designers". This is because of their popularity amongst graphic designers.*

If you want to overpaint an area of watercolor with a pale color, don't use thick coats of color as when the paint dries it will damage the picture's surface.

As gouache doesn't contain much binding agent it remains soluble once dry, this means that if you apply a color over a previous layer, the new paint may pick up a hint of the color beneath.

However, the technique of painting on wet is not very advisable when using tempera. before applying the next coat ensure that the previous one is completely dry. That said, if you wish to make gouache that is insoluble in water when dry, you can do so by pounding it together with a liquid solution that contains 4% gelatine and 2% formulin; this medium will also work well with oil based media. As well as combining gouache with watercolor, it can also be used with acrylics, which makes for a richer paint, the media are adaptable and impermeable, in other words they can be applied layer upon layer without corrupting the colors of the previous layer.

56

57

Fig.56. **Jane Avril leaving the Moulin Rouge** *by Toulouse-Lautrec. Gouache on card (Wadsworth Atheneum, Hartford).*

Fig.57. **In the Moulin Rouge: the start of the quadrille** *by Toulouse-Lautrec. Oil and gouache on card (National Gallery of Art, Washington).*

Painting with Gum Arabic and Casein

Gum glues like these: gum arabic (originating from plants) and casein (originating from animals) are suitable solvents for watercolor and gum based paints. They can however be mixed directly with the pigments, this option offers additional media to work with. Gum arabic is a resinous substance which is clear or yellowish brown and it is formed by the vitrifying sap of various species of acacia that grow in North America and Sudan. It often contains a small amount of glycerine which gives the substance more of a shine.

Gum arabic is a fairly viscous liquid which can be bought in flasks or in its natural state as a solid resin. In this case you need to leave it submerged in water for 24 hours while it dissolves. The impurities such as particles of bark or earth can be removed by filtering the liquid through cloth. When this preparation is added to powdered pigment a very thick paint medium is formed, which can be used to create a whole range of interesting effects and textures.

Given the characteristics of this medium it works well when combined with inks, although it is also possible to use it with watercolor or *gouache*. The gum arabic solution can also be used as a binding agent for watercolors and for this reason these media can be found in combination in some works. If gum arabic is added to watercolor or ink it increases their brilliance and gives them more body. It can also be used with these media by adding it as a veil and giving an interesting texture to the finish, it acts as a varnish and gives a lasting shine to the surface. Gum arabic can be used with: Chinese ink, watercolor, *gouache* and tempera.

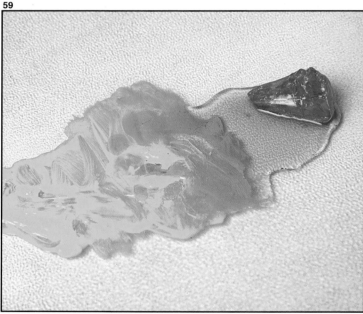

Fig.58. Gum arabic is available as a solid. In order to make the binding agent you simply have to submerge the block in a container of water and leave it a few hours to dissolve.
Fig.59. Once dissolved it has a rich texture similar to that of honey. To prepare the mixture of gum and powdered pigment use a glass or marble surface.

Casein has been widely recognised as an effective glue for centuries; it is a liquid form of albumen which is found in milk, and it is obtained by precipitation using acid. Casein needs careful preparation as follows: put 300 grams of casein into a container and add it to a litre and a half of water. Leave it for 12 hours for the casein to soften. The following day heat the contents of the container for an hour at 60°C. Then add 60 cubic cm of ammonia and heat it for a further hour, this time at 90°C. Now all you have to do is add the powdered pigment to the glue-like mixture. Paint made with casein has a matt appearance and a rich consistency. It works well combined with media that are not water soluble so it can be used in conjunction with oils and their derivatives. A coat of casein paint becomes very hard and taut when it dries.

Because of its resistance to water and the elements, this type of paint works well with fresco and tempera.

Fig.60. Casein is a milky substance which, when combined with pigment produces a highly resilient paint. This can be used in combination with oils.

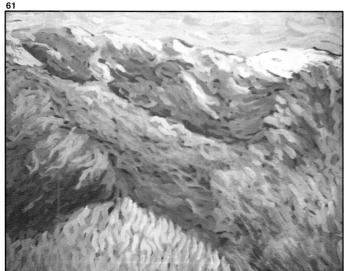

Fig.61. Painting with casein has one setback, the colors of the paint change dramatically as they dry. Of all media, casein shows the greatest weakness in this respect. **Landscape in Cadí** by Gabriel Martín (artist's private collection).

Fig.62. The casein based colors tend to have a pale appearance so they are often used in conjunction with oils which are used to introduce bolder colors. **Calle Provenza** by Gabriel Martín (artist's private collection).

Instinctive Techniques: Frottage y Grattage

In this next section we are going to see artistic creativity encountering a free and intuitive art form; which uses Instinctive Techniques developed to a great extent by the surrealists, in particular by Max Ernst who is considered the creator of *frottage*. This technique became so popular that today it is included in a variety of more common pictorial techniques. The artist places a thin piece of paper over any surface that is interwoven or that has a highly defined texture and rubs with a soft pencil so that an image of the surface beneath appears on the paper. So, the artist can create a huge variety of shapes and textures through this very simple process which relies on the pattern of the material they have chosen. These textural patterns can be found on surfaces such as wood, clothing, wickerwork or wooden carvings. Try experimenting with different media and colors to test the different effects and color variations that you can achieve.

Grattage is a variant of *frottage*, which involves placing the already painted paper over an uneven surface and scraping back the paint so that a negative of the texture below is created. Techniques which rely on scraping back or scratching the surface are derived from similar oil painting techniques.

Sgraffito is another related technique which also allows the artist to create new effects and textures. Sgraffito is one of the most effective and straightforward techniques when working with wax, it consists of using an awl to scratch away to reveal a surface that has previously been covered with a layer of color. This effect can also be achieved with encaustic paint, but here, the wax allows you to create the drawing by simply scratching the surface. Once the first lines have been scored, the artist has to try and imagine a composition that will incorporate the textural effects that have been obtained, which, aside from the patterning made by the *frottage* he should try to create a simple figurative composition.

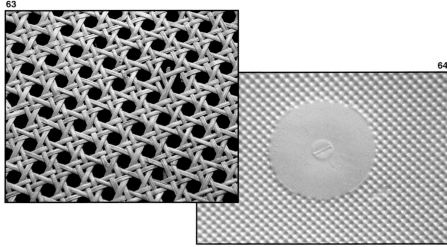

Figs. 63, 64 & 65. You can take an impression of any surface that has a distinctive relief. Any shape or interweave of materials can catch the artist's eye: a section of wickerwork (fig.63), the base of a plastic plate (fig.64) or a wooden carving (fig.65).

Fig.66. Max Ernst, as well as being the creator of frottage, incorporated gratage into his surrealist oil paintings such as this one, **Spine Forest** *(Beyeler Gallery, Basle).*

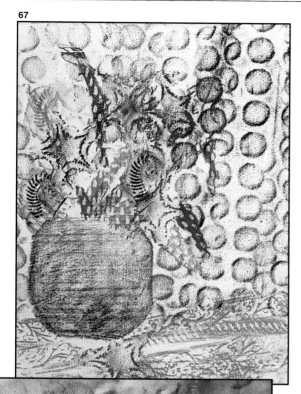

67

68

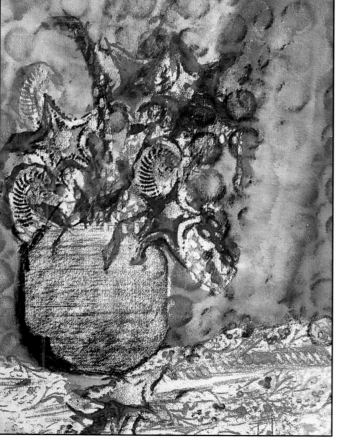

69

Figs.67, 68 & 69. The artist Bibiana Crespo demonstrates to us how to create a composition through the use of frottage: Firstly, she takes a piece of thin paper and takes rubbings with wax on different surfaces (a tree trunk, a lino floor, a cheese grater, etc...) (fig.67); once the basic drawing has been created, watercolor is applied with a brush to the background in order to make the flower arrangement stand out more (fig.68); finally she further distinguishes the shapes of flowers and adds final details and touches of color to give the work a more finished look (fig.69).

Mixing Acrylics, Latex paints and Oils

70

Plastic or latex paints can be classified as a sort of tempera, their only difference being that the gums that they are made up with are polymers: vinyl or acrylic. The outstanding versatility and quick drying time of acrylic and latex paints make these two of the most popular choices for mixed media techniques. Artists often combine these media with watercolor, *gouache*, oil, ink, pastel or charcoal, enabling them to maximise the expressive qualities of each medium.

The main advantage of acrylics is that they dry extremely quickly, in comparison with the slow drying through oxidation/ oxidisation of oil paints. Acrylic and latex paints are soon dry because of the quick evaporation of the water contained in the binding agent, this leaves a coat of paint that is pliable and there are no significant alterations of color as the paint dries. However, there are some setbacks; one of which is that the quick drying of the paint is not always advantageous, although it seems such a bonus, it restricts the artist who has to work faster, when working with oils you are

71

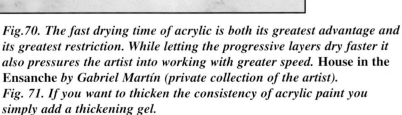

72

Fig.70. The fast drying time of acrylic is both its greatest advantage and its greatest restriction. While letting the progressive layers dry faster it also pressures the artist into working with greater speed. **House in the Ensanche** *by Gabriel Martín (private collection of the artist).*

Fig. 71. If you want to thicken the consistency of acrylic paint you simply add a thickening gel.

Fig.72. Acrylics allow you to paint using a broad range of styles from total abstract to detailed figurative work. **Paperweight** *by Beverly Hallam (National Museum of Women in the Arts).*

able to keep retouching for a far longer period of time.

Because of this a slow evaporating liquid can be added to lengthen the drying time.

Acrylics do not have a thick consistency which makes it difficult to create textures or use them for impasto. There are only two ways around this problem: mix the acrylic with a thickening gel which gives the paint a heavier consistency or alternatively paint the first layers in acrylic and use oil paints to add the finishing touches, impasto and volume. The latter is the most commonly used option. But, remember what we said earlier, oil can be applied over acrylic but not the other way round. Acrylic has little hold on the oil paint surface.

By contrast, paints made with latex have a far better hold and can be applied on top of oils if the surface has dried correctly (do not apply latex onto oil that is too fresh). Latex is also one of the most effective glues to stick paper or other three dimensional objects to create *collage*. However, if you are going to be using watercolor it is best not to use latex on paper as once the glue has dried it tends to leave white patches on the paper's surface. Watercolors do not hold well over this surface.

Because of the satin finish of acrylics, latex without pigment can be applied to the surface of the painting and it acts as a varnish. In this way the surface acquires brilliance and shine.

Figs.73 & 74. Miguel Olivares is an artist who often uses acrylics in combination with collage. In his paintings he develops colorist themes inspired by fleeting images from his trips to Morocco and its fruit stalls. **Djemâa el-Fna** *Nº1 (fig.73) and* **Watermelon** *(fig.74) (both from private collections).*

74

Painting with Encaustic and Crushed Marble

Of the whole range of media, encaustic is probably the hardest to apply. In the first place this is because it is a paint consisting of hot wax, the pigment has to be mixed with the wax which is kept liquid by heating it on a hot ring. The artist needs to work quickly as the wax only stays liquid while hot and it solidifies quickly once it is applied to the support.

Once applied however, it is easy to retouch; this can be done with a heated metal tool even if the wax is set. Note that by contrast, this practice is totally inadvisable with an already dry oil painting. Many artists have used wax and oil paints in combination as the two media work well in conjunction. Encaustic paint does not yellow with time, it doesn't oxidise or contract, it is not water sensitive and it creates very interesting visual effects.

Encaustic paint can be applied to any support combined with any media, including on murals although a layer of plaster should be applied first, this serves to seal the support of the paint from the wall.

In a similar process, the cooled liquid wax or a compound of wax soap diluted in water can be applied like a tempera paint or even mixed with casein.

75

76

Fig.75. In this encaustic painting by Richard Gersti Group with Shönberg (Kamm collection, Switzerland), you can admire the textural effects and blurring created by this combination of media. The principal qualities of this way of painting are the impasto effects and the blurred forms that are represented in an expressionist manner.

Fig.76. Pure wax, i.e. wax untreated by any chemicals, is the basis of encaustic painting. The properties of wax allow the artist to obtain many different types of textural effects and impasto on the picture's surface.

Besides wax, there are also other highly effective methods of creating texture and relief in a painting. Crushed marble stands out as the most important of these.

If latex is mixed with crushed marble (which is sold by weight) a paste-like substance similar to cement is produced. With a spatula and a resistant bristle brush, the paste can be spread to add texture to the composition where it is required (tree foliage, billowing clouds, a rocky mountainside...). The support must be flat, i.e. resting horizontally on a table. Once the paste has been applied, let it dry for a few hours. When it has dried you will see that it is paled to white. Now you can paint over the relief surfaces either with acrylic or oil in the same way you would on any surface. This technique is not advisable with watercolors, aniline or *gouache* given the complete inability of crushed marble to absorb water. The color will not take hold and will form droplets just as water does on any non-absorbent surface.

77

Fig.77.Latex is a milky liquid which,when mixed with crushed marble becomes a thick paste.This can be applied on the surface of a canvas to create texture and low relief effects.

78

79

Fig.79. **La Provenza** *by Hans Berger (Kunstmuseum Solothurn). The brushwork and the impasto effect helps to create a greater sensation of depth and relief in a painting.*

Fig.78. You can see in **Landscape in Cadí** *by Gabriel Martín (artist's private collection) the characteristic textures created by use of marble* *powder. The relief is smoother quite unlike the impasto produced when using the encaustic technique.*

Fresco and Tempera painting

80

Mural painting is yet another creative process which can be considered as a forum for trying out combinations of mixed media. Fresco is probably the most commonly used medium for mural painting. The paint is made up of lime resistant pigments in powder form, which are applied onto a freshly made surface of mortar made up of lime and sand. Fresco needs to be applied swiftly and skillfully as the paint can only be applied while the mortar is still damp. The pigments are simply diluted in water and applied straight to the support. Once absorbed by the crystalline form of the lime, the atmosphere's drying effect completes the process through chemical reaction which causes a film of calcium carbonate to form over the surface of the paint. This binds the colors with the surface they have been applied to in such a way that once dry they become insoluble in water. In this case the lime acts as a binding agent. The colors of washes applied to damp gesso will appear faded. But, if the artist works on a dry support, the layer of paint applied to the surface appears as a glaze, however, this is not an advisable method as the color does not hold well. It is adequate for simple graphics and highly stylised images, and for colorist techniques. It is quite the opposite of the paste-like applications of paint in oil paintings.

If you want to work on dry or mix fresco with other media it is advisable to bind the pigment with gum or glue which will produce tempera. This is why fresco is combined with casein or egg tempera.

Tempera is often used for retouching and must be used in a semi-solid rather than liquid form. For the best results it should be applied with a round ended bristle brush. It is inadvisable to paint on murals with watercolor or *gouache* (even less advisable to use oils or oil based paints), the short term results are disastrous. Fresco and water based colors are two media best kept apart.

Fig.80. The vaults and aisles of churches tend to be the most suitable place for fresco painting. Above you can see an unfinished composition by the **St Francis Master** *(crypt chapel of Saint Francis of Assisi).*

*Fig.81. During the Italian Renaissance, Giotto painted frescos of such great skill and quality that his genius remains uncontested. In the blue of the sky you can distinguish that the fresco was worked on over a series of days (***Saint Francis receiving stigmata, Church of Saint Francis of Assisi***).*

81

The traditional method of tempera painting consists of binding pure pigments with egg yolk and distilled water.

The resulting medium is similar in consistency and quality to acrylic so, not surprisingly, it is applied in much the same way although the resulting appearance of the work is different. The one setback is that the artist has to work swiftly as egg yolk dries very fast. This problem can be overcome however, by mixing oil in with the tempera which lengthens the drying time. You will remember that Van Eyck mixed oil with tempera with very effective results. If you want to use tempera as a base and use it in combination with oils remember that the support that you are going to paint on should be primed with rabbit skin glue before the base colors are applied. This is a simple process: mix the rabbit skin glue with water, the proportions should be one unit of glue to ten units of water, and leave it to stand overnight. The following day, heat the mixture until the glue dissolves, add a little Spanish White and stir it in. Apply it to the support and leave it to dry overnight. The following morning everything is ready for you to start painting.

Fig.82. Tempera paint has egg yolk as its base. When pigment is added to it, a pastelike paint is formed which crystalises once it is dry.

82

84

83

Fig. 83. Tempera is the ideal medium to paint the translucent veils of color used to capture the faces of the Gothic and Renaissance Madonnas. See how the brushstrokes are virtually invisible, distinguishing the skill and delicacy with which the flesh of the figure has been recreated. **Madonna** *by Fra Angélico (museo Thyssen-Bornemisza, Barcelona).*

Fig.84. For centuries, tempera has been used in combination with other media, for example the tempera and oil combination above in **The Annunciation** *by Gentile Bellini (museo Thyssen-Bornemisza, Madrid).*

Ephemeral materials

There is a series of art techniques concerned with creating artworks that are not lasting or permanent, these works are defined by the fact that they are not made to last and they are created with objets trouvés or ephemeral materials. These types of works were at their creative peak during Art Informel, so called because they were influenced by the movement of non-figurative painting which started in Europe in the 50's.

This movement was based on the outcome of the artist's need for personal expression and the rough way in which their materials were often handled as a result.

It is often said that Art Informel is a material-based approach, as artists often used crushed marble with latex or clay, which gives it a heavy consistency which in turn allow for techniques such as incisions, lumps, cracks etc. The artists best known for this technique are Jean Dubuffet and Antoni Tapies.

Using recycled materials and gluing objects to the pictures, adding new types of industrial paint, made of latex mixed with sawdust, sand or straw, these new methods made the artist's choices ever more versatile.

In this chapter I aim to encourage you to investigate; play with materials, take up the challenge of creating your own mixes of materials, apply all sorts of objects to the painting's surface, unconcerned by figurative representation. Try to assimilate these exercises as necessary exploration for its own sake rather than being concerned by the finished work. The materials and techniques used should not be seen as an end in themselves but rather as a starting point for investigating your future work, in other words this will be a testing ground for the development of techniques that you can later use in figurative works.

The art world is constantly developing at such a rate that the artist who looks at new ways of applying and combining media and techniques will find new ways of exploiting and adapting new ideas to suit his own personal style.

85

86

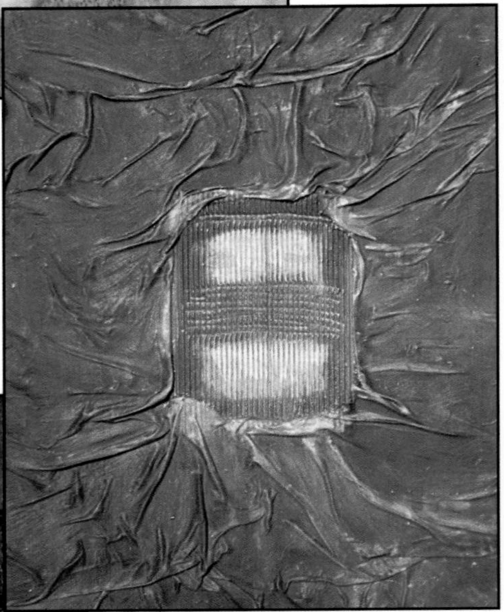

87

Fig.85. **Untitled** *by Gabriel Martín (private collection). Mixed media; latex paint, oil and crushed marble.*
Fig.87 **The Alienator,** *by Kurt Schwitters (museo Thyssen-Bornemisza, Madrid). Collage and oil paint with a range of different materials on a rigid board.*

Fig.86. **The Liceo Opera House** *by Gabriel Martín (private collection of the artist), made with recycled objects (red material and card).*
Fig.88. (opposite page). **White with Red Stains** *by Antoni Tapies (Mª Lluïsa Lacambra, Barcelona). The artist has created a rich texture by applying rich impasto layers of crushed marble and foam.*

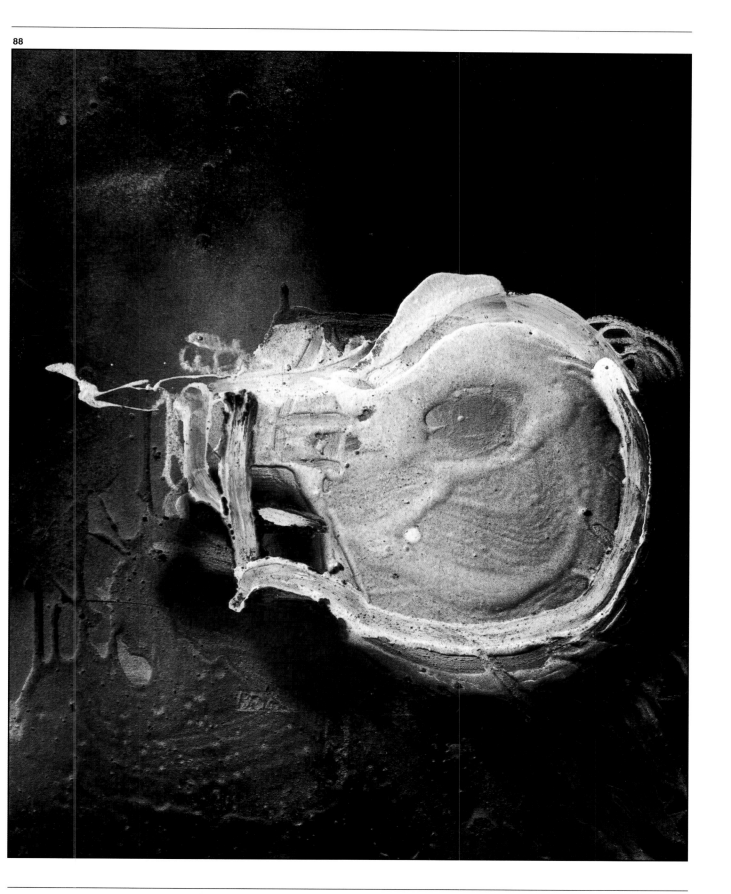

PRACTICAL EXERCISES

In the following pages you will find a series of practical exercises which will take you step by step through a range of subjects painted with mixed media by professional artists. Each exercise is explained by concise text, with instructions and advice so that you can easily follow the development of each step. A series of numbered guidelines have been supplied to be used with some of the exercises explained in this chapter, these are to act as aids when following the creative process of the artist. All that remains for you to do is turn over, get started and give yourself adequate time for each exercise.

Creating a Still Life using Collage

89

We are going to start with a simple exercise: creating a still life with *collage* and latex paint which is made up of pigments and latex glue. The resulting image will not just be a convincing copy of the subject it must also be a pleasing image. Bibiana Crespo, a highly skilled artist and art teacher is going to be giving us some valuable advice.

As you see, the subject is simple: a bottle, some glasses containing ice cubes, a wooden box, some dry laurel leaves and a newspaper. It is important that a variety of interesting objects are used and that there is a geometric balance created by them (fig.89). As well as latex and pigments, you will also need colored paper, an illustrated newspaper and some scissors.

Start with the largest surface areas (the bottle, the box and the background). Choose your paper dependent on its tone and cut out the shapes (fig.90). You can use any type of glue or gum to apply the paper, but as we are combining *collage* with latex paint it would be easiest to use latex as a glue. It dries quickly and can be easily applied with a brush. Keep sticking pieces of paper, superimposing them until you have made a plan of all the objects in the still life (fig.91). As you can see, you can combine strident colors (like the background behind the bottle) with other duller colors, in this way the large planes of color contrast with the smaller details such as the bottle top, the glasses or the ice cubes (represented by two stamps). What better than a piece of newspaper to represent the newspaper featured in the subject, this also introduces printed graphics to the composition.

Continue to add details in the same way, progressively adding further details to the forms; a piece of light blue paper beneath the box, some bits of yellow plastic for ice cubes, cuttings of a magazine cover for the laurel leaves and finally a piece of cream colored paper for the bottle's label (fig.92).

90

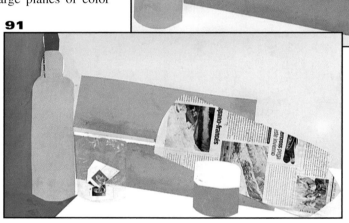

91

92

Fig.89 The subject has a subtle geometrical balance (the cylindrical bottle, the rectangle of the newspaper...) which makes the exercise easier to carry out.
Fig. 90. Start working be recreating the biggest surface areas with large pieces of paper.
Fig.91. Continue by adding details onto the cuttings in place, further defining the forms; including each object that makes up the composition.
Fig.92. Add more colors to the image: cuttings of magazine photos for the laurel leaves, yellow ice cubes and sky blue beneath the box.

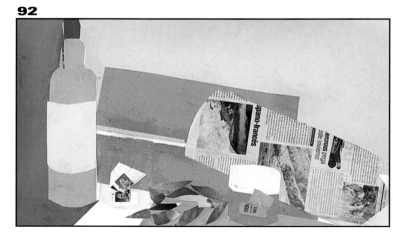

93

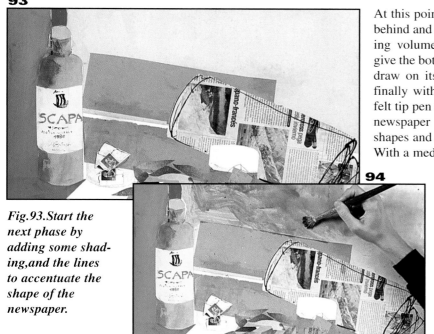

94

Fig.93.Start the next phase by adding some shading,and the lines to accentuate the shape of the newspaper.

Fig.94.Latex paint changes the look of the background to soften the contrasts in the work.

95

Fig.95.Work on the contrasts between light and shade on the inside of the box and define the outline of the glasses.

96

At this point we must leave the building blocks of collage behind and begin focusing on the pictorial aspect, by creating volume, shaping objects, casting shadows etc. First give the bottle volume by shading it with burnt umber, then draw on its label with an aquarelle pencil and ink, and finally with a small container of chinese ink similar to a felt tip pen add lines to further distinguish the shape of the newspaper (fig.93). The image is built using contrasting shapes and curved lines.

With a medium brush make good the background: apply a diluted grey wash with a slightly blue tinge which will lend the image a more pictorial aspect (fig.94).

Continue to add volume to the different objects, adding shading to the flat, uniform colors of the paper so that the painting begins to appear more three dimensional. Add color to the laurel leaves, alter and shade the glasses and their contents and add volume and details to the wooden box with ochre and Burnt Umber to build up contrasts of light and shade (fig.95).

The work is almost finished, all that is left to do is to cover the entire background with the same grey wash, give the wooden box further color and details and concentrate on the foreground; further defining the crystal of the glasses and the laurel leaves (fig.96). As you can see, the finished work is not even vaguely realist. This is more of a productive exercise in composition than a beautiful, delicately worked painting. And this is exactly how the use of collage should be viewed, as a thorough exercise in observation which allows you to abstract the form down to its simplest components. You have to know how to observe, consider and appreciate how the shapes are made up. Once you have carried out various exercises like this, you will see that it becomes progressively easier to extract the basic forms of the model, to capture the subject and its composition.

Fig.96. Here is the finished work. This has to be seen more as an exercise in composition than as a picture of great artistic value.

A Street Scene in Watercolor and Anilines

97

In this exercise we are going to mix two media with similar properties. I am referring in this case to traditional watercolors and anilines (also called liquid watercolors). As you know, traditional watercolor gives a more grainy effect, while anilines are more saturated and similar in appearance to colored inks. Óscar Sanchís will be showing us how to go about this exercise, he is an expert at painting street scenes. The scene he has chosen is a boulevard in a small Swiss town. As you can see the subject is full of color and variations of light and shade, some of the buildings have facades decorated with balconies, cornices and turrets (fig.97). Why not take up guideline Nº1 and follow the artist's progress step by step as he develops the exercise.

The first thing that needs to be done before even beginning to paint is the primary sketch which is obviously done in pencil. I would recommend a 2B pencil for this purpose. You only need to trace the contours of each of the figures and do a line drawing of the facades, there is no need for any kind of shading at this stage (fig.98). If you prefer you can use guideline Nº1 as a basis.

In order to start painting you will need a special palette of anilines at hand. If you look at fig.99. you will see how the mixing palette is similar to that used with watercolor, the difference being that the tray sections are deeper as anilines are more liquid.

98

99

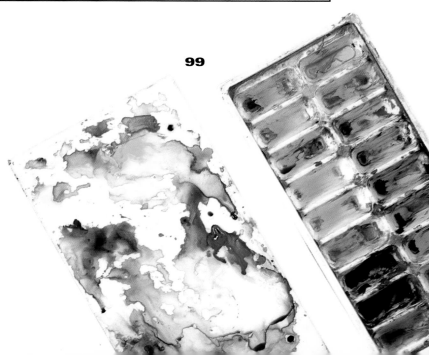

Fig. 97. The subject that we are going to paint is a small tourist town in North East Switzerland.
Fig.98. The first step, as always with watercolors, is to make a line drawing which sets out the subjects of the composition. If you prefer this process has been started for you in guideline Nº1.
Fig. 99. This is an ideal palette for anilines. The difference between this and a watercolor palette is that this has deeper sections to hold the more liquid paints.

So, let's start by working on some background details with anilines. Take a medium brush and mix a little Lemon Yellow, Ultramarine Blue and sepia, instead of mixing them in the palette apply them directly to the paper, adding them to each other so that they mix, creating an interesting effect (fig.100).

Take a paintbrush with short bristles like the one in the image and add a deep brown on dry. The resulting lines are not crisp and you can make out the texture of the paper which helps create a textural variety in the work (fig.101) At this stage you want to keep the brush fairly dry.

Next, paint a wash on the patch of sky

in the top left-hand corner. Continue right away to spread a pale touch of cobalt blue to the wash, a little ultramarine blue to the roof of the house and, with a fine brush, trace some horizontals in sepia.

You can see this sepia color in the illustration, anilines painted on wet spread irregularly over the surface of the paper (fig.102). If you paint with the support slightly tilted, as the artist does here, it is better to work from the top downwards so that any drops of paint that may be produced by painting on wet will run downwards. Start working on the facade.

100

101

102

103

Fig.100. If working on an inclined board, start by painting from the top so that any drops of color that run can be caught.
Fig.101 With a short bristled brush you can create an endless amount of textural effects which will reveal the grain of the paper.
Fig.102. When painting on wet, the colors mix and run across the surface of the paper. Have a look at the umber colored patch in the top right part of the already painted area.
Fig.103. The facades of the old houses painted with anilines are surprisingly rich in color variation. The washes are fresh and have a certain tendency towards orange and violet. These are to be the two dominant colors of the work.

You can now start to prepare the traditional watercolors on the palette, they will serve to widen the range and richness of the color scheme although they should blend in the same way as has been achieved so far. Note how the facades make up an abstract background of colors, windows and balconies seem to emerge from the background, defined by a few simple lines (fig.103).

Copy the artist. Take an old toothbrush, dip it in watered down aniline (Emerald Green in this case) and flick a spray of paint over the painted surface by scraping the bristles back with a fingernail. These effects serve to introduce further textures over the background washes and break up the plain flat areas (fig.104). You can see how effectively this technique works on the lower half of the buildings' facades. Now begin to work on the crowd in the foreground, don't worry about facial features and details (fig.105). Simply build up each figure with a few brushstrokes. In this style of painting you have to synthesize shapes and details (fig.106). In the following images (figs. 106, 107 & 108) you can see how the artist develops the figures.

104

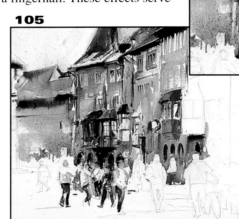

105

Fig.104. Paint flicking creates new textures, it gives surface of the picture a grainy look.

Fig.105. Work on two areas at once, the passers-by in the foreground and the facades of the buildings on the right.

Fig.106. The figures have to be simplified, they are painted with a few simple strokes, without details or facial features.

106

TIPS

- When painting on dry with a short bristled brush, work the brush repeatedly and briskly over the paper, it may not be enough to draw the brush over the paper just once.

- When painting with anilines on wet do not let the colors run too much. You can control this by tilting the support in the opposite direction to the way the drops are running or absorbing excess paint with paper towel.

- If you want to open white spaces in aniline paints rub a little bleach onto the area and the color will vanish after a few minutes.

107

108

Fig.107. The pavement of the street has been painted using a selection of colors which have been flicked over the surface.
Fig.108. There are many ways of creating contrasts and textures. Here the fingertip is used to good effect.

109

The freshness and spontaneity of approach is clearly evident as you study the different details in the foreground. There are many effective ways of creating interesting effects: scratching with a fingernail, opening white spaces with a *scapel* or, as in this case, smudging the wash of paint with your fingertip (fig.108 opposite). After completing the last step which is to give texture to the road by spraying it with anilines (green, lemon yellow and a little sepia), you can consider your exercise complete. Compare your work with the one by Óscar Sanchís above. It should be as similar as possible to the original. If the final mix of colors is not an exact equivalent, never mind, as long as the work has captured a certain fresh, spontaneous look. Sometimes people wrongly suppose that a sparsely detailed unfocused foreground such as the one shown above, gives the impression that the work is unfinished. Don't make the mistake of adding too much detail to the figures and the facades as the result will appear fussy. Keep in mind the synthesis of the whole work. You should have achieved a lively picture through the skilled application of patches of color, summarizing the features of the subject without going into too much detail (fig.109).

Fig. 109. Here we have the finished work. It is a painting of considerable artistic merit, with brilliant colors and expressive qualities.

Painting a Fortress in Casein and Oils

Now we are going to attempt a painting using a combination of casein and oil on the same support. As you may remember, the casein solution acts as a glue and it is very suitable for painting backgrounds when painted onto a firm support. We are going to use a wooden board as a support for this exercise. Before starting to paint however, let us consider how the colors should be prepared. The painter and sculptor Francesc Mas will be demonstrating to us how to do this and then showing how they are applied to create a pleasing work in casein and oil.

Casein can be bought in a powdered form from any good shop selling artist's materials. When you need to make up the glue, put 50g of powder into a bowl and add 100 cubic cm of hot water (fig.110). Gently stir the solution. The liquid will whiten and become thicker as you stir it with a teaspoon. Let the solution stand overnight. The next day heat it for an hour at 60°C. Add a little drop of ammonia and return it to the heat, this time at 90°C.

111

Mix this binding agent with powdered pigment, in this case the artist is using Titanium White (fig.111). Stir the mixture with a teaspoon until it becomes a creamy paste. Next, store the resulting mass in a container and get ready to prepare another color (fig.112).

The measurements I gave earlier for making up the binding agent were just for a single color, however, it is better to make up a large quantity of binding agent and keep it in a container, in this way it can be used to make a larger quantity of colors.

The subject that Francesc Mas has chosen for this exercise is a view of the fortress of Carcassonne, a beautiful Medieval walled city in the South of France. (fig.113 opposite). Before beginning your preparatory drawing you must prime the support. There are no types of paint that are applied directly to wood without any sort of preparation. As casein acts as a strong glue it can be used as a primer. For this preparation add a little Spanish White and ammonium carbonate to the solution that you have used to make the paints (don't be surprised if the solution starts bubbling; it's perfectly normal).

Fig.110. Firstly, add water to the powdered casein and stir it with a teaspoon.

Fig.111. Add the solution to the pigment so that the glue acts as a binding agent for the paint.

112

Fig.112. Once it has been stirred a little, the mixture develops a creamy consistency. Put the mixture into a container and repeat the same process with the other colors.

113

Fig.113. The subject is Carcasonne, a picturesque town in the south of France, which presents a historic landscape that is famed for its medieval buildings

Fig.114. After priming the solid support with a little casein and Spanish white, make a charcoal sketch of the subject, just like the artist has done.

114

115

116

117

Apply the substance to the surface of the wooden board and let it dry for half an hour.

Now your support is ready to be painted on. With a piece of charcoal make a schematic drawing of the subject as the artist has done (fig.114). You can use the same paint hypen brushes for the casein paint as for oil paints. I recommend the firmest hog bristle brushes.

Start by extending a uniform wash over the darkest color zones, starting with the tower and the wall in the foreground and certain faces of the architecture in the middle ground (fig.115). As you have already observed no doubt, casein paints cover the surface with an opaque layer and there is a considerable variation between freshly applied paint (which is much darker in color) and the same paint once it is dry. You will find this the greatest drawback to painting with casein. Keep this factor in mind as it will have an effect on the finished result.

So, as you can see, the painting is developed in the same manner as a *gouache* or tempera painting.

Next, continue by working on the pointed roof of the turret in the foreground, using a little Ultramarine Blue and Titanium White. Use a lighter shade on the left and a slightly darker tone on the right. Your aim at this stage is to recreate a cylindrical object as you add volume to the tower with touches of light and shade. Do the same with the pointed roof of the lower tower on the left (fig.116).

In order to avoid simultaneous contrasts, add the vegetation along the foot of the wall (Verona Green, yellow and Emerald Green). See how the paint is applied in vertical brushstrokes.

Fig.115. Start by painting the large grey planes of color in the foreground, but don't forget the background, the painting should be worked on as a whole and not in sections.
Fig.116. Turn your attention to the pointed roofs of the towers in the foreground, painting them in blues

and violets, using a lighter blue on the left and a somewhat darker tone on the right.
Fig.117. When painting vegetation it is important to consider the direction of the brushstrokes to create a more realistic patch of grass.

59

It is common practice when painting vegetation to use upward brushstrokes, imitating the direction of growth, this also creates a textured effect which adds to the interest and variety in the work as a whole (fig.117 previous page).

Let's return now to the stone architecture; the walls, battlements and towers. Work on the foreground, adding details such as the windows, the texture of the stonework, shading and giving further volume to the conical towers. The area in the distance is going to remain far more schematic, with flat washes and softer colors. Shapes and profiles are less detailed because of the distance. There tends to be a clear distinction between the more detailed foreground and more diffuse and sketchy distance.

It is worth noting that although the colors in the foreground and the distance are the same, those in the distance are somewhat softer, the colors are less intense (fig.118).

Now paint the sky with a wash of Ultramarine Blue and Titanium White. As you will see in the example, this creates a cloudy aspect with a slight reddish tinge. We are not going to give the clouds any further definition but leave that until the end when we use oils, which are far more effective for retouching colors. The sky has been painted by applying two flat washes which have combined, the top wash is of a slightly darker blue than the one beneath.

On the left of the castle, add a patch of blue to suggest a distant mountain range. Add a second wash to the middle ground to intensify the color of the patch of grass. Work on this detail keeping the general color scheme in mind, colors should not be seen in isolation, the tone should tie in with the rest of the picture. The picture will then appear to have a tonal and chromatic coherence (fig.119).

Continue by covering any blank areas on the canvas with a succession of washes, altering the colors, adding little patches of vegetation and adding a little ochre to the patch of grass. Finally add the final touches to the smaller tower (fig.120).

Fig. 118. This is the moment to focus on textures and color values. Look carefully at the tower and the wall in the foreground and see how, little by little, the buildings in the distance are taking shape.
Fig.119. The sky is an important part of any composition, as it is one of the factors which determines the atmosphere of the scene.

Fig.120. Continue by adding details to the vegetation in the middle ground with a touch of ochre, and a deeper green for the bushes and the group of cypresses on the far right.
Fig.121. Oil is more loosely handled and gives brighter colors so it has been used to add chromatic variation to the clouds and to pick out details on the distant buildings and the apex of the main tower.

122

Fig.122. The finished painting is very impressive. As you may remember, this combination of mixed media when tempera is used in conjunction with casein or oil is an ancient practice. It was used extensively by Van Eyck.

TIPS

- Fat free milk diluted in a little water can also be used as a thinner for casein.
- Don't be impatient. Wait till the colors dry to see what their true tonal values are. Don't be tempted to speed up the drying process by using a hairdryer, the heat could crack the paint or warp the wooden support.
- When applying oils to casein it is important that the casein is totally dry.

Now is the moment to take up the oil paints and make the composition more lively and colorful. Start by working on the sky: with a flat brush add tiny reddish dashes and thick strokes of white and sky blue which build up the clouds enriching the variations. Then take some Burnt Umber and a touch of Ultramarine Blue and lighten the mixture by adding white. Apply the color to the walls of the castle in the distance. Finally, with a slightly greyish sky blue add the finishing touches to the tower in the foreground (fig.121 previous page). And here is the final result (fig.122). See how the composition has been considerably altered by the introduction of dabs of oil paints: which have added further dynamism and contrast. If you look at the stonework in the foreground you will see how the blocks have been suggested, don't make the mistake of

attempting to recreate them in photographic detail. Remember the value of synthesis. Observe how some details have been left unfinished; the apex of the towers, the vegetation below... Painting a picture is not about representing every compositional element in photographic detail, but about capturing the elements of variety and interest that will hold the viewer's attention. This is achieved through synthesis and sketchy hints of detail, so that the viewer can interpret and reconstruct the subject in his mind's eye. Finally it gives the work a certain freedom which allows the viewer their own interpretation of these fragmented details.

Another aspect to bear in mind is the style in which the sky is painted, given that it is not always blue, but can vary from gray to pink to cream. I recommend that from this point you take

plenty of photographs of subjects and paint them as we have done in this exercise.

Painting a Seascape in Watercolor and Gouache

The artist Maria Ángeles Agesta is going to use watercolors and *gouache* to create a clear, vivid composition in cold colors. This photo of an attractive harbor scene taken on the fishermen's quay in Barcelona (fig.123) is what we will be using as a model to demonstrate the use of these media step by step.

You can now take up guideline N° 2 and complete the drawing started there (fig.124).

Start by applying a dilute wash to the top part of the paper with a large brush. With a medium brush start by painting the sky. First apply a violet color well diluted with water to the top of the sky-line and let it blend with a watery yellow introduced along the horizon line (fig.125).

Next, add in the quay and the mountain in the background with a violet blue. The mountain, because of its distance from the viewer should be lighter blue (fig.126). Add a wash of very diluted paint to the sea which should counteract the dazzling effect of the vast white spaces. As you can see, the range of pale colors used to paint the sea blend together when applied on wet. The colors of the sky are reflected in the sea. Study fig.126 and see how the surface of the water reveals shadows and reflections. These are caused by the shifting colors reflected by the sea and the purplish shadows cast by the boats. Once the initial wash has dried, start detailing and clarifying the group of boats in the distance (fig.127).

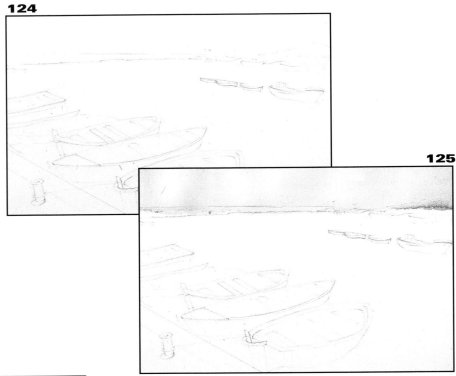

Fig.123. This fisherman's quay in Barcelona is going to be the model for our next exercise.

Fig.124. With a N° 2 pencil, make a preparatory sketch which positions each one of the elements which we are going to paint, alternatively, take up guideline N°2.

Fig.125. Start with the sky. Paint on wet with a little Ultramarine Blue, yellow and orange so that the colors blend to form this impressive effect.

Fig.126. Now turn your attention to the quay that you see further into the distance and to the mountain on the right, describing them with a purplish color. Now paint the water's surface with a very pale blue which reflects the colors that were used to paint the sky.

Use a fine sable brush. Try to give the craft shape and volume but don't go into too much detail because, as you know, objects seen from a distance appear faded and indistinct. (fig.128).

Now concentrate on the boats in the middle ground, using slightly stronger colors. I suggest you use the same brush as you used for the boats in the distance, but this time try to define the forms a little more, adding new colors to the picture (deep orange and blue tones) and keeping in mind the outline of the craft and the shadows they cast onto the water (fig.129).

The first stage of the exercise is almost finished. All that's needed is to add some washes of color to the boats in the foreground and the corner of quayside that can be seen in the bottom left hand corner. Use flat washes of sky blue and ochre. Strengthen the deepest shadows with indigo and deepen the shadows cast onto the calm sea (fig.130). Now it is time to leave the watercolors and take up the *gouache* paints. As a rule, you will find that watercolor palettes are too small to work with *gouache*, so I recommend this artist's method.

127

128

Fig.127. As you can see, the artist has worked from top to bottom, starting with the furthest planes.
Fig.128. With a fine brush, detail the boats that are furthest away, don't make them too defined, keep them sketch-like.

129

130

Fig.129. You should introduce more color when painting the boats in the middle ground to creat sharper contrasts, and the shapes should be defined so that they appear closer, as stated by the laws of recession.
Fig.130. Apply the initial washes of watercolor to the boats in the foreground to give the subject a base color onto which you can start to work with gouaches.

Take two plastic plates, the sort you might take on a picnic; arrange the palette of colors on one and use the other to mix colors (fig.133).

The properties of *gouache* are similar to those of watercolors, they can even be used wet on wet. In this case however, it is harder to achieve the atmospheric effects that the artist has used in the farthest picture plane. So, start by working on the boats using flat washes of color, keeping the color uniform and avoiding shading or impasto (fig.131). At this point it is important to allow the media to blend, they can even be used in the same wash. To paint the decks of the boats follow the example of the artist who has made the colors paler by adding white. If, instead of adding white paint, water is added to make the color paler, the resulting paint would be semi-opaque and milky, while the white paint thickens the resulting paint, the color is denser and more opaque (fig.132).

Cover the previous watercolor washes applied to the boats with some layers of white *gouache* and use the same paint to highlight other details and to bring out the areas where the reflections of the light are strongest. Add the smaller details such as the rope and the mooring post with a fine sable brush. The artist is in total control of the media in this work, she has combined the transparent layers of watercolor with the matt, opaque *gouache*, to create a subtle interplay of color and tone. This evokes a sense of atmosphere in the work.

131

132

Fig.131. With the **gouache,** *start to mould and give volume to the closest group of boats. As you will observe,* **gouache** *is dense and opaque.*
Fig.132. The properties of **gouache** *enable the painter to obtain a foreground that is more contrasted than the middle ground and an atmospheric background. The use of contrast in the work creates a sense of depth in the picture.*
Fig.133. Use a plastic plate as a palette and another to mix colors.*

TIPS

- Your first washes should be in watercolor, then apply the *gouache* on top, not the other way round as *gouache* has better covering power.
- When painting with *gouache* it is better not to apply the paint as impasto, gouache is brittle and will crumble if the paper is creased.
- Similar to watercolors, if *gouache* paints dry out they can be revived by adding a little water.

133

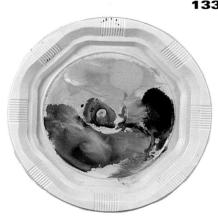

134

135

Compare the final result (fig 134) with your own work and see if you have also managed to capture the contrasts and shading of the boats in the foreground through your use of *gouache*. They should have a more highly defined, compact and dimensional look in comparison with the softer, less defined transparency of the boats in the middle ground and distance which have been painted in watercolor. Although the artist has used mixed media you will see how the color range carries across the media, creating a harmonious balance of colors. The same should be the case with your work.

If you have not been taking this color harmony into account the result will surely be a broken range of colors including some colors that clash with the general tone of the painting. If this is the case, I would give the exercise another try, focusing on this aspect.

Fig.134. See how the work has taken on a more schematic appearance in it's final stage. The finish has been left undetailed so that you can fully appreciate the difference between the two media.
Fig.135. If you wish, you can introduce new textures and further shading into the work, as the artist has done in the final stage.

An Interior using Chinese Ink and Gum Arabic

In order to carry out this exercise we first need to find a straight-forward subject with deep colors and sufficient dark areas to paint in Chinese Ink. The subject has to be chosen to bring out the best qualities of these two media. The subject found by the artist is an interior with a couple of sofas, a lamp and a glass coffee table. The scene is bathed in natural light which comes in through a large window on the left of the composition.

There is no need to prepare your colors beforehand when carrying out this exercise. All you need is a selection of pigments at hand which can be mixed with gum arabic as and when you need them. Óscar Sanchís will be demonstrating how the work progresses step by step. If you want to follow the development closely take guideline Nº3 as a starting point.

Having completed the sketch begun in the guideline (fig.136) apply the color (fig.137). Prepare the colors as you go. You can do this by putting some gum arabic on a plate and adding the pigment that you need. When the gum arabic and the pigment are mixed a foamy mixture is produced which slides smoothly over the paper, creating interesting textural effects. You can start painting the background with clear, transparent washes of ochre, blue and orange. While the first wash is still wet, add some deeper shadow round the lamp with Burnt Umber.

While you let the background dry, take up a medium brush and add in the vertical stripes on the sofas, use an umber shade diluted with water. These lines should be curved so that they describe the form and volume of the sofa. Paint the glass table on wet, first with a blueish wash which should be blended with a touch of ochre and indigo in the darkest corner. Leave a white strip to suggest reflection. Finally paint the legs of the table with a mix of indigo and burnt umber, outline the lamp with the same colors so that it stands out from the background (fig 138).

Take the same mixture that was used for the table legs and work on the sofas, avoiding overlapping the color with the vertical stripes you painted earlier. Let the white of the paper show through, don't totally cover the surface with paint. If you look closely at the work you will see that the coloring of the sofa is a blend of little touches of yellow, blue and ochre (fig.139 next page).Keep working on the far wall,

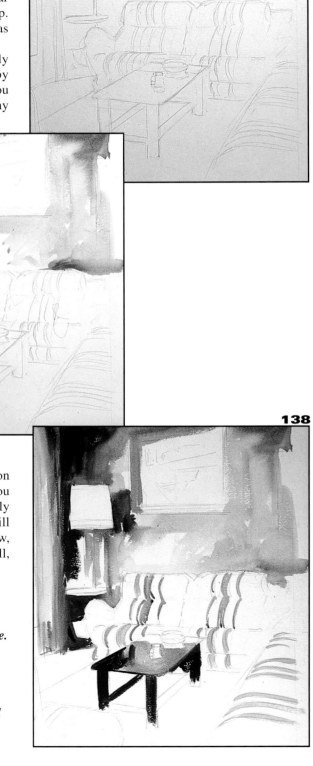

Fig. 136. The pencil sketch is complicated because of the perspective. If you want, you can use guideline Nº3 to help with this stage.
Fig.137. Start applying a wash to the wall in the background with bold, transparent colors which blend on wet across the paper's surface.
Fig. 138. Continue by adding further colors to the background and paint the glass surface of the table using wet on wet, creating the illusion that it is transparent.

introduce a wash for the carpet which will act as a base for the patterned design, and attempt to vary the tone and brightness of the colors. Add in the frames of the pictures that are hanging on the wall and add shading to the lampshade to give it volume. This can be done by shading it with an orange color, throwing the right side of it into shadow with deeper tones working the colors so they are lighter in the middle and the brightest area is on the left (fig.140).

The thickness of gum arabic paints means that a wet paintbrush easily picks up the color, and creates denser washes than those you would see with traditional watercolor. You are sure to notice this as you continue work on the sofas or as you make a scribbled design on the carpet. Remember the words summary, insinuation, sketching. Study the carpet and see how patterning is lighter on the part that is closest to the light source, and how it darkens further away. Try and imitate this (fig.141).

As you will observe, paints that use gum as a binding agent tend to contain a certain amount of glycerine which give a satin finish to the colors. Now add in the pictures in the background, keeping it simple and schematic, so that the white space is covered (fig.142 following page).

139

140

141

Fig.139. Paint the sofas using Burnt Umber with a touch of indigo. If you look carefully you will see many nuances of color that are interwoven to enrich the painting. This is a characteristic resource of Óscar Sanchís.

Fig. 140. Add washes of Ochre, Sienna and Burnt Umber to the carpet, keeping the tones brighter on the left and darker on the right where they are farther from the light source.

Fig.141. We have reached the stage where nearly all the areas of white paper have been covered, it is now easier to asses more accurately how the colors relate to one another without being put off by false contrasts.

The exercise is almost finished. Continue to work little by little on the depth of the shadows and the colors and start concentrating on adding certain details such as the glass ashtray and the lighter that are sitting on the table, the red fringe around the lamp-shade, etc. Build up and enrich the contrasts and values by reworking the previous wash in certain areas (fig.143).

This is the moment to add the deepest shadows for which you will need the black Chinese Ink. Intensify the shadows using a Japanese ink brush, apply the ink to give further depth to the work. While doing this, work with the same brush, tracing some lines on the back wall and outlining certain objects such as the edges of the table and the outline of the sofa in the foreground (fig.144).

As you will have observed by now, adding gum arabic to pigment or ink increases its brilliance and body. It also creates an interesting texture.

If you look closely you will notice that certain patches have been left white, so that the grain of the paper is revealed, this gives a further texture to the painting.

142

143

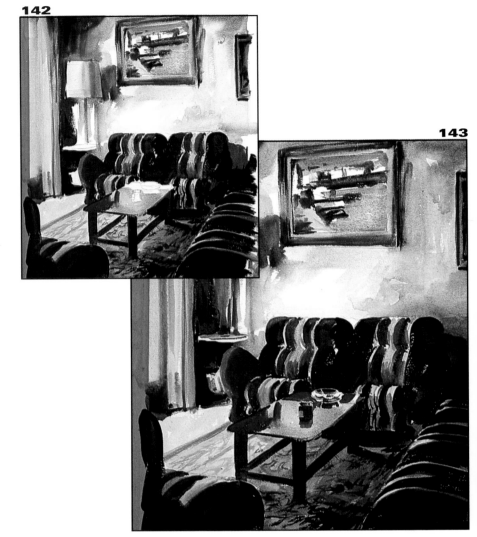

Fig.142. Paint the picture hanging on the wall using free schematic blocks, ensure that the colors chosen harmonize with the rest of the composition.

Fig.143. Spend a few moments studying the painting and correcting errors, building shadows, adding details and half tones etc.

Fig.144. Take up a Japanese paintbrush and a bottle of Chinese Ink. Roughly outline certain objects, intensify the shadows add textures and lines etc.

144

TIPS

- If you want to create further textures you can scrape at the paint before it dries.

- Try not to work and rework colors onto a particular area as it may smudge.

145

If you have followed this exercise closely you will surely have spotted that this method of mixing and applying colors is similar in some ways to working with oils or acrylics although the result is more transparent. Don't underestimate the key role of the white paper. Consider the importance of combining deep colors (like the sofas and the corner in shadow) with areas where the colors must be applied in more transparent washes, areas where the white of the paper "breathes" (the curtains on the left, the back wall and the glass table) (fig.145).

Fig. 145. This is the final result of a perfect partnership of two media that have so much in common: gum arabic and Chinese ink. if you are used to painting with traditional watercolors I recommend that you try these media, you will be surprised at what they have to offer.

Flowers in Watercolor, Pastels and Aquarelles

The illustrator and watercolorist Josep A.Domingo is going to paint a floral arrangement using a combination of media well known by keen artists: aquarelle pencils, traditional watercolors and pastels. As the aim of these demonstrations is to help you learn through practice, why not take guideline Nº4 and follow the development of the picture as the artist takes you step by step through the process explained below.

This time I suggest that you take a bunch of flowers like this, you should be able to get hold of some easily. It is important to source our subject matter from our every day surroundings. Generally if there is a birthday in the family or some special occasion, the house is full of flowers that make a good subject to paint (fig 146).

What the artist has done here is to start by making a drawing in aquarelles. If you are hesitant about tackling the subject right away in aquarelles you can always make a seperate sketch and trace it using aquarelles (fig.147). You could also use the guideline that I've just mentioned. If you do start with aquarelles make sure to add each detail using a suitable color right from the start. In any case, the basic shapes making up the subject and the main color zones should be clearly defined from the beginning.

Try to shape and introduce color values to the image, keeping the shading light (building things up as you go along) so that the colors appear very pale. You only have to apply the pencils softly without pressing too hard on the paper. As you can see in this sketch, the artist has decided to omit any references to the background and is focusing all his attention on the main subject (fig.148).

Take a medium paintbrush, wetted with water and begin to apply a wash onto the sketch. Start with the largest flowers in the centre and continue working outwards until you reach the perimeter of the composition. You can work the water soluble colors with the brush, making sure to wash the brush each time you move on to another color. Try to keep the colors clean, avoid letting them mix: there is no need to apply the brush hard on the surface or the water will run (fig.149 following page).

Fig.146. You will always find subjects to paint in your immediate surroundings, like a bunch of flowers for example.
Fig.147. There is no need to make a primary sketch in graphite pencil you can start your composition right away with aquarelles. If you prefer you can use guideline Nº4.
Fig.148. This is how the bunch of flowers looks when drawn in aquarelles. See how the lines are faint, there is hardly any contrast or intense color.

When you have applied water to the aquarelle sketching, take up the aquarelles again and add further details to the first impression: add a touch of yellow to some of the flowers, Ultramarine Blue with Payne's Grey to the darkest shadows in the centre of the bunch..., these new colors should compliment the colors already present in the initial sketch (fig.150).

Take up a thick paintbrush and introduce a wash in violet watercolor to the background. Avoid painting over the outline of the vase and the mat beneath it. Extend the wash to create an aura of color around the base of the vase. Reserve a vertical strip of white to suggest the table's reflective surface, waxed and smooth (fig.151). You have to get the wash right first time, you cannot make any alterations without smudging and spoiling the general appearance of the picture.

Next, study fig.152 on the following page where you will see how the painting progresses; you will see that all the colors have now been introduced although the contrasts are not very evident. The vase has been painted using a dilute Olive Green, little reserves of white have been left, to suggest the exture of the glass.

149

Fig.149. Take a wetted paintbrush and carefully dilute the colors, so that the lines drawn by the aquarelles are combined with the tentative brush-strokes of the wash.

150

Fig.150. Having overpainted the aquarelle sketch with water take up the aquarelles again and intro-duce further colors into the composition.

151

Fig.151. As the contrasts are built up they lend the image more volume. Apply a violet wash around the glass vase, detailing the reflection at this stage.

71

Some of the leaves, stems and petals have also been highlighted. As you can see, the picture has acquired some shading, sufficient to give a certain impression of volume but not enough to consider the work finished.

So, what's needed is more contrast, from now on we will work in pastels which will give us the opportunity to make the tones and the shapes bolder.

Before starting to use pastels it is absolutely crucial to let the paper dry. If you work on paper that is still damp you will end up with powdered masses of color that are difficult to get rid of. First, start by lightly detailing the out line of the petals with Vermilion Red. Add a little dark green into the leaves and smudge the color with a finger. Highlight the orange parts of the flowers with yellow and intensify the color of certain leaves and stems with blue, delicately tracing them with thin lines which should not be smudged (fig.153).

With a violet colored pastel reinforce the background wash, smudging the color with a fingertip, avoid smudging the vase or the mat. See how the violet is not applied evenly, but that it is more concentrated to the left of the subject. To get rid of excess powder, tap the paper sharply down on the table or if you prefer, you can blow directly onto the reworked parts.

Leave the most delicate leaves and the smallest details until last; you need a steady hand and a steady eye.

In the finished work (fig.155, following page) there are certain characteristics of drawing and others of painting revealed. The delicate washes are fused with lines from the aquarelles and the pastels.

152

Fig.152. As you can see, at this stage the contrasts are not very sharp.

Fig.153. With the pastel sticks work on the volume of the subject, sharpening up the shape of the petals and creating stronger contrasts.

153

154

Fig.154. It is not enough to draw and shade in pastel, it is important to merge the colors with the previous washes. This can be achieved by smudging and blending the colors with your fingers.

TIPS

- When drawing with aquarelles keep in mind the direction of the lines of shading. The lines should coincide with the shape and relief of the object.

- If you haven't worked with pastels before this exercise I would familiarize yourself with the medium first by trying out some patches of color and shading and smudging them with a finger.

- Before dissolving the aquarelle with a wet paintbrush pause to consider what effect you are looking to achieve.

155

If you found the drawing phase with aquarelles difficult, I suggest that the next time you try this technique you start with a general wash over which you can add the color values and develop the work in the same way that you would if working with watercolors. Aquarelles should not be complicated to use, provided that you control the application of water when diluting them. You will soon find yourself at home with this medium once you have discovered its secrets. If, once you have finished the work, you see that one of the colors does not stand out sufficiently, it may be because of the lack of contrast between that color and the colors that surround it. Build in color contrasts even if it means altering the colors from those that you see in the model.

Fig.155. Here is the final result. It works well. Observe how little contrast there is between the three different media that were used, they are a perfect combination.

Painting a Lake in Acrylics and Oils

Yet again we are counting on Josep A.Domingo's skills to help us with this exercise. He will be painting a scene in acrylics and oils. The subject is a peaceful view of a lake in Catalonia on a summer afternoon (fig.156). To paint this scene in acrylics you will need the following colors, Burnt Umber, Chrome Green, Cadmium Yellow, Cobalt Blue, Ultramarine Blue, Golden Ochre, Olive Green, Emerald Green, Raw Umber, Vermilion and Titanium White. You will also need a selection of flat bristle brushes and a sable brush for details.

156

Take guideline N°5 and complete the drawing (fig.157). First add some delicate touches in Ultramarine Blue to the darkest areas where the color is most intense. Some artists always paint in the shadows in a violet color particularly in the open air as the light conditions can change rapidly (fig.158). Continue by adding the main themes of the landscape with a mixture of Golden Ochre and a little Olive Green with Ultramarine Blue. At this stage the colors should be applied in a diluted form, making cautious progress to avoid covering the entire sketch with opaque paint. These dilute colors serve as a base for the following washes (fig.159).

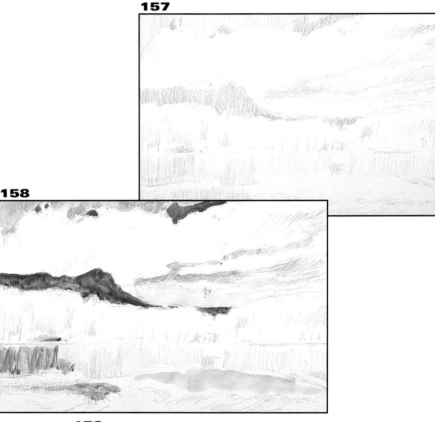

157

158

Fig.156. The subject for this exercise is a Catalonian lake with calm crystalline waters which reflect the trees along the shoreline.
Fig.157. Take guideline N°5 or make a sketch with a semi-hard pencil. This doesn't have to be a line drawing as any sketching will eventually be covered by opaque paint.
Fig.158. Paint delicately at first then with increasing boldness, first introducing washes of blue in the clear patches of sky, the distant hills and the lake.
Fig. 159. Continue adding washes and toning down the white of the paper. You will notice that at this stage the washes are transparent, applied in a similar manner to watercolors.

159

Add a little orange in the middle ground and some Olive Green and Cobalt Blue in the lower half of the picture. What you have to do now is keep adding further layers over the initial washes. Reproduce the colors of the vegetation, upside down on the surface of the water, to create the reflections. Start to sculpt the clouds in soft pinks and blues, painting them using delicate layers of paint, overlaying the colors to create an atmospheric effect (fig.160).

Keep working, complete the deep blue hills and the clouds gathered in the sky, then move on to the foreground and middle ground. Observe how, as the more intense colors are introduced (the violet in the sky, the oranges in the vegetation), the painting gains volume, depth and intensity (fig.161).

Now turn your attention to the surface of the lake. See how the artist has painted the reflections of the trees along the far margins of the lake. He uses a range of colors similar to those used for the trees but the range is darker and colder. You will also notice that where the house is reflected, the artist has left a white space which projects vertically over the crystalline surface of the lake. All these reflections are painted with strong vertical brushstrokes. The foreground is still roughly defined, the washes are uneven and of varying thickness. Try to imitate this effect (fig.162).

160

Fig.160. Add the first contrasts and color gradations to the initial washes. In this way the image progressively develops using the colors taken from the original.

161

162

163

Fig.161. Work on the image as a whole, developing a richer blend of colors so that the clouds and the middle ground are intensified.

Fig.162. See how the reflections in the water recreate the same shapes and colors of the vegetation on the margin of the water. This can be achieved by simply extending the strips of color vertically downwards.

Fig.163. With a fine sable brush, develop the distant reflections and the ripples that appear on the water's surface in the foreground.

The next part of the exercise is more complex and requires all your powers of observation. To paint the ripples on the water's surface in the foreground you need to look carefully at how they are created. In order to reproduce them take up a fine sable brush, a little sky blue, and patiently trace the radiating ripples.

With the same brush, using a darker Olive Green, continue working on the ripples by adding little patches with a series of parallel lines of irregular lengths (fig.163 previous page).

Continue by adding details in the middle ground with hints of Olive Green, oranges, yellows and reds. For this, use a fine bristle brush. The brilliant dashes of orange bring out the middle ground, while the blues and pinks of the clouds on the horizon make them recede. In this respect, colors are another important factor when it comes to creating depth in a composition (fig.164). Bear in mind that any alterations of color that you make to the vegetation need to be imitated in the reflections on the water's surface.

Look closely at the clouds, their initial sketchy appearance has been refined, the distant hills are clearly defined.

164

Fig 164. If you want to highlight the house all you need do is intensify the colors of the vegetation surrounding it and it will stand out because of the increased contrasts.

165

Fig.165. This is the result of the work in acrylics. From this point we will work on the texture of the composition using oil paints.

166

Fig.166. Work an impasto across the clouds with a flat brush, giving them more body.
Fig.167. Do the same with the vegetation in the middle ground. The texture of the crowns of the trees works well and is complimented by the brilliant colors of the oil paints.

167

TIPS

- Paint some of the details with dense colors to contrast with areas of diluted and subdued tone. This will bring the composition to life.
- Before applying oils to the acrylic paints be sure that the acrylics are completely dry, if they are damp it is highly likely that the surface will start cracking in a few days.
- Remember that oil is always applied to acrylics and never the other way round. Acrylics do not have enough hold to be painted over oils and after a few days they will start to peel off.

The sharp profile of the hills has the effect of projecting them towards us, however, this effect is contradicted by the smooth texture of this plane (fig.165 earlier page).

Now you can leave the acrylics and take up the oils. By applying an impasto of colors, you can create textures that enrich the composition by adding relief and depth. It is vital to vary the paint's consistency to create interesting textures. To do this, the artist takes a small flat brush and adds some initial layers of impasto to increase the body of the clouds (fig.166 previous page). As you will see, oil paints have a more brilliant appearance than acrylics.

The abundant use of oil impasto applied in the middle ground has the effect that the trees are projected towards the viewer, they become the focal point of the composition. The use of oils also allows you to liven up the colors of the middle ground by adding irregular brushstrokes to the vegetation. If you look closely at the detail (fig.167 previous page) you will see how distinct the two media are from one another.

You may well have had problems creating the reflections in the lake and the ripples in the foreground. Unfortunately it is hard to advise you further as there are no specific rules that make these effects easier to capture. All I can suggest is that you look carefully at the way in which the artist has combined and applied the colors and that you endeavour to do likewise.

If you find yourself struggling with a similar difficulty when painting outdoors, you must rely on meticulous observation and attempt to transfer the information that you see directly onto the paper. Turning to the combination of oils and acrylics, you shouldn't have any problems with these two media as, despite their different consistency, they are not dissimilar in terms of the way they should be handled and applied. Perhaps the only drawback that you may come across is the speed at which the acrylics dry, you are under pressure to work swiftly, you may be pushed for time if you want to mix colors on wet.

Fig.168. This is the finished composition, which skillfully combines the qualities of the two media: the quick drying and excellent covering power of acrylics and the freshness, texture and brilliance of the oil paints.

168

A Landscape using Wax crayons and Turpentine

In the following exercise we are going to use wax crayons and turpentine, which is used to dilute the crayons, smudge the colors and create interesting pictorial effects. The artist Manel Grau Carod will demonstrate how to work with these techniques. The subject is a mountainous landscape with well defined colors and rich vegetation.

As usual, we will start by making a pencil sketch with a 2B pencil (fig. 170). If you prefer, you can use guideline N°6. First we begin with the sky; take a crayon of Ultramarine Blue and work it gently across the paper. Then add a layer of light turquoise over this, applying the turquoise with more vigour (fig.171). Continue by applying a medium paintbrush dipped in turps so that the colors mix creating an irregular wash similar to a watercolor wash. (fig.172). Introduce one or two new colors to the sky, fuschia and violet have been used here on the right.

Now turn to the rocky mountains in the distance. Add a little Prussian Blue to the rocky outcrops, Yellow Cadmium to the area bathed in sunlight, outline the rocks shade the cliff face on the right with violet, and add a little Permanent Green to the vegetation on the eroded slope. You will see that although the colors appear pale from the start, the artist softens the lines of wax crayon by rubbing at them with a paintbrush dipped in turps (fig.173).

The background has a bluish tendency typical of the atmospheric effects of distance, the characteristic discoloration occurs as the subject recedes from the spectator.

Now concentrate on the middle ground, drawing with the wax crayons and diluting with the turps; here you can also try blurring the colors by using the wetted tips of your fingers (fig.174 following page). See how aware the artist is of the direction of the shading: diagonal in the foreground, or more irregular in the rocks of the middle ground. (fig.175 following page).

Compare the middle ground of fig.176 with the previous phase, and you will see that gradually the artist is beginning to finalize the lines and details: the outline of the vegetation on the right in Burnt Umber and Bile Green, the cracks and fissures of the rocky cliff face on the left in violet and orange. This has made the middle ground stand out better now from the hazy hills that appear in the distance (fig.176 following page).

169

Fig 169. The subject is a typical sunny scene of the Catalonian Pre-Pyrenees. It stands out because of the sharpness of the details that make up the scene and the density of the vegetation in the foreground and middle ground.

170

171

172

Fig.170. The first stage is to draw the subject with a 2B pencil, there is no need for it to be a schematic sketch, wax crayons will cover the pencil lines more effectively than watercolor.

Figs.171 & 172. In these two images you can see how the artist develops the simple lines traced in wax crayon into an undulating wash that covers the sky.

Fig.173. Work on the far hills, first applying the contrasting colors and then merging them with the use of the paintbrush.

173

174

175

176

Once the turps washes have dried, rework the painted areas, now using bolder lines to suggest the different textures.

Working with a heavy medium such as wax crayons can result in bold expressionist work, which allows for the liberal and effective use of overlaid meshes of strident colors (fig. 177). You will notice the rich amalgam of different colors in this detail. Keep adding intense colors, increasingly warmer and brighter. Strengthen the impact further by applying them in irregular lines which describe the irregular texture of the bushes and trees: small agitated strokes that suggest the shadows and volume of the subject.

You may have overlaid too many layers of color or applied too many lines which have converted areas into dull patches with little tonal definition. Don't worry however, something can be done about it. All you need do is take a knife or a *scapel* and you can remove all excess wax with one single scrape of the surface. When the surface is clear again you can paint over it, this time taking care not to make the same mistake. Don't use the same approach to the background as you have with the foreground. Here, washes and veils of color should always be used as they give the effect of distance and atmosphere, in fact if you work too much detail into the background then the resulting picture will lack depth and appear overworked with overcrowded tremulous lines (fig.178).

Fig.174. The middle ground is colored with ochres, pinks, umbers and greens, i.e. with warm colors that contrast with the cool colors employed in the distant mountains. Fig.175. The white of the paper has to be covered by a succession of layers of shading which are diluted with turps. In this way you will be sure to avoid letting any patches of white paper show through. Fig. 176. The volume and texture of the work is not simply created through contrasting and diffusing the colors, texture is also achieved by the direction of the shading.

177

178

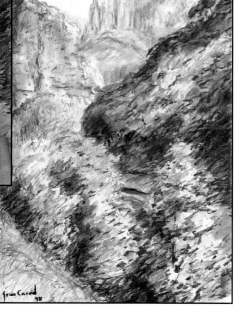

Fig.178. Put aside the turps and concentrate on finishing the foreground, draw a mesh of agitated abrupt lines to intermingle the colors on top of each other. Study the final result.

Fig.177. In this detail you can see how the shading of different colors is superimposed. You will also notice the inclusion of unusual colors such as light blue, pink, red and violet.

TIPS

-Keep in mind that wax crayons are not suitable for small format works or for pictures that require great attention to detail, the crayons are too thick to enable you to make clean, precise lines.

A Landscape in Oils with Crushed Marble

In this next step by step I will explain how crushed marble and latex can be used to add texture to compositions, and how this process can be used in combination with oily media such as oil paints. In the following pages I will show you how to prepare the materials and use them to obtain interesting textures and effects that you can use in your work. This time, the task of demonstration falls to Ester Llaudet, a skilled artist and teacher.

Before making a start we have to prepare the mixture. For this, you will need the following materials: half a kilo of crushed marble, a kilo of latex glue, a broad palette knife, a fine oil paint brush, a wooden stick, a plastic plate and, lastly the support that we are going to paint on (in this case a canvas ready primed and mounted on a wooden frame). First, study the model which you are about to paint and decide which of the textures you want to accentuate. When this is decided, prepare the crushed marble. Put a fair amount of latex onto the plastic plate (fig 179). Add the crushed marble and stir the mixture with a stick or a plastic spoon until it forms a paste-like substance (fig 180). Scoop up the mixture with the palette knife and spread it across the surface of the canvas. Try to recreate the textures of the foreground and middle ground with the brush. Continue with the same process; this time describing the branches of the tree using the fine brush or the palette knife that you used to carry over the mixture to the canvas. Leave a blank untextured space where the group of distant hills and the sky are to be painted (fig 181). Once you are satisfied with the textural effects that you have created, let the crushed marble dry for two to three hours until hard. Then you will be ready to paint.

Ester Llaudet has taken this landscape as a model, a combination of woods and farmland is ideal subject for creating interesting effects of texture (fig 182 following page). Compare the photo of the landscape with the canvas prepared with crushed marble (fig 183 following page). You will see that the reliefs and the textured areas correspond with the textures represented in the model.

The support is ready and we can begin

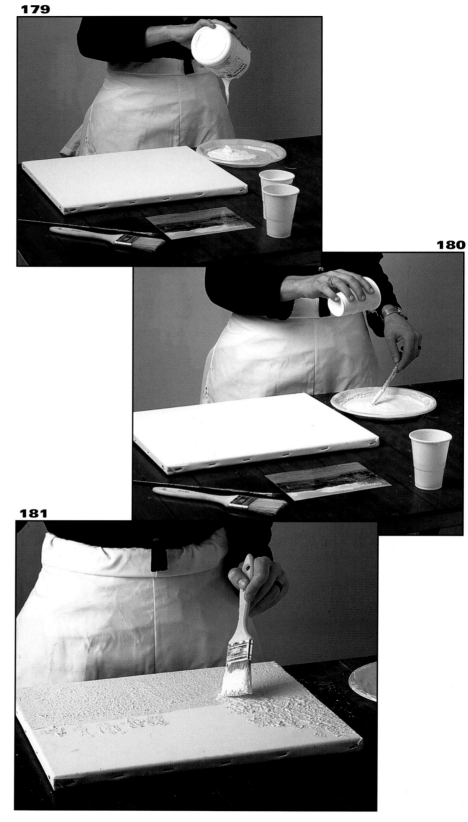

Fig. 179. First add the latex to the container that you are going to use to make the mixture.

Fig.180. Add the crushed marble and stir it with a stick until it becomes a paste-like mass with a thick consistency.

Fig.181. With the palette knife, add the mixture of crushed marble onto the support, creating textures and effects from the earliest stage of the work.

to paint. As you have done before, I suggest that you follow the process with the step by step demonstration below which describes the development of the picture.

You will need a complete palette of oil paints which you can get hold of in any art shop, although I suggest that if you have time you should make your own with powdered pigments and a little linseed oil.

Start by painting the large field in the foreground with Cadmium Yellow, a touch of Permanent Green and Yellow Ochre. The color should be applied slightly thinned with turps, so that the paint leaves runnels of color and irregular patches in the background, which adds to the granular effect of the crushed marble. With a little Emerald Green and a slightly smaller flat brush, apply the shadows of the line of the trees in the middle ground and the grass strip at the bottom of the canvas (fig.184). Paint the slope in the center in English Red and with Gall Green add the vegetation that is growing at the foot of the mountain in the distance. These are not definitive colors as yet, but they serve as a base and cover the white ground which helps to avoid the problem of simultaneous contrasts (fig 185).

Continue to work on the middle ground, shaping the slope with a little Zinc White and English Red. Next, concentrate on the distant mountains with a grey made up of unequal parts of Ivory Black, Prussian Blue, Titaniuum White and Carmine. You will see that the mountains are represented in two subtly

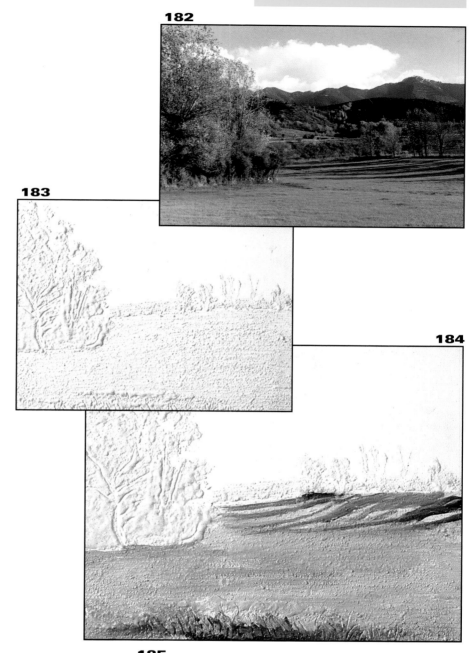

Fig.182. The model re-creates the textures of the vegetation; branches and trunks that show through the leaves, the leafy crowns of the trees, extensive grassland etc.
Fig 183. This is the result when the paint has been left to dry for a few hours. Compare this with the original photo of the model.
Fig.184. Paint a yellow wash diluted with turps over the field in the foreground, then add the shadows made by the trees and bushes onto the slope using Emerald Green.
Fig.185. Continue working on the middle ground using irregular agitated strokes in an effort to further increase the textural effects of the dense foliage.

different shades: a lighter gray for the patches catching the light and darker gray for areas in the shade. As this is in the distance it is better not to add too much detail; describe the area with more synthesis (fig 186).

With a fine brush, detail the vegetation in the middle ground, giving shape and color to each of the trees with a touch of indigo, Hooker Green and Burnt Umber. Rework the colors of the field with a veil of Permanent Green. At the same time, add touches of color to the line of trees in the middle ground and do the same with the grassland and bushes on the bank that separates the two fields (fig.187).

Note how the forms of the trees in the middle ground present a contrast because of their coloring and shapes. Now turn to the tree in the foreground on the left and apply Cadmium Yellow thinned with plenty of turps to cover the white of the crushed marble. This color is used as a background to overpaint the colors and textures of the foliage. Start by adding a series of more intense washes although somewhat diluted, with Emerald Green, Indigo, English Red and deeper Cadmium Yellow to highlight some of the bushes (fig 188).

Capture the play of light and shade across the tree on the left by working on it with Green Umber mixed with a touch of indigo. As you apply the color you will notice how it gathers in the runnels and textured parts made by the crushed marble. Detail the crown of the tree on the left with a darker color over a lighter foundation, creating the effect of a play of light with the darker green over the yellow. Paint some of the branches in the top of the crown with Ochre and Vermilion. At the same time, darken the base and trunk of the tree and add further color to the bushes there, the trunk and some of the branches (fig.189). So, this is the final result, having added

186

187

188

189

Fig.186. The distant hills are easy to paint, all you have to do is work with two subtly different shades of grey to describe the lit and shaded planes of the mountainside.

Fig.187. With a fine brush, the artist has added some details. I suggest that for once you don't follow his example, given that this medium does not allow for highly detailed work.

Fig.188. Paint the tree on the left, firstly with a diluted wash which eases the brightness of the white, then add some more intense colors to the bushes that grow at its base.

Fig.189. The artist has worked on the crown of the tree giving it more volume and using more intense colors and he has highlighted the shape of the trunk and the main branches.

the final touches to the sky and the clouds. See how the artist has eased the yellow of the field with layers of Burnt Sienna, representing the shadows projected by the trees in the middle ground. Touch up the profile and the light and shade of the mountainside, you will notice that the steeper sides have been retouched with green and darker grey. If you have tried to interpret the branches of the trees and the texture of the vegetation with greater detail you will have found it a hard task given that crushed marble is rough and unaccomodating, making intricate work impossible. Also, continual work on this surface quickly wears out finer paintbrushes, because of the friction as the brush is applied to the rough surface of the crushed marble. When working on this material it is advisable to use paint thinned with turps rather than thick

coats of color. In this way the colors seep into the granulated texture and add further textural effects to the composition (fig 190).

Fig.190. The painting in its finished state, despite the rough, hard texture of the crushed marble, the painting has a rich variety of color and texture. The combination of oil paints and crushed marble is currently one of the most popular mixed media techniques.

TIPS

- When painting over crushed marble it is better to use a selection of bristle brushes as they are more hardwearing. If you use synthetic or sable brushes you will be concerned when you discover how quickly they are worn by the friction of the crushed marble's granular surface.

- Try to be decisive from the start about the texture and effects you want to create when the crushed marble that you've applied is still wet. Once it has dried it hardens it cannot be altered, the only way to rectify a mistake is to make up some more of the mixture and add it to the first layer.

190

Painting with Oils and Encaustic

Painting with encaustic technique is one of the hardest media for a student of art, however, it does make for some surprising and spectacular results. The texture produced is unique and unmistakable. There is no other method of painting which will produce similar results and for this very reason I would encourage you to learn this technique despite the initial challenges and complications and soon you will be rewarded by good results.

As you already know, encaustic technique consists of painting with wax paints made liquid by heating. To carry this out you will need a hotplate, a large casserole dish and a smaller saucepan that sits in the casserole dish which is full of hot water, and a spoon to stir the wax. When the water is hot, drop the pure wax into the saucepan (fig.192). When the wax has totally liquefied, you must leave it on the heat, don't remove it just turn down the heat a little so it is warm enough and doesn't start going solid again.

Whenever using encaustic technique it is always best to have a metal or ceramic palette, so that you can put it on a warm surface (such as a nearby radiator) and the wax colors will stay liquid. As for the oil paints, they can be home made or from a tube.

Before you start, prepare the palette on a warm surface adding to it the color range that you are going to use. Situate it close by to the saucepan with the liquefied wax.

Let's begin. First select a suitable subject. It should have a variety of prominent textures, just like this alley in Pals, a small town in Catalonia, a subject where a variety of colors and textures are to be found in the stones (fig.193). The support should preferably be rigid. In this case the artist, Ester Llaudet, has used a wooden board primed with Spanish White, although if you prefer you can use canvas like the ones used for oil painting.

191

Fig. 191 Before starting to paint you have to heat the wax in a double boiler.

192

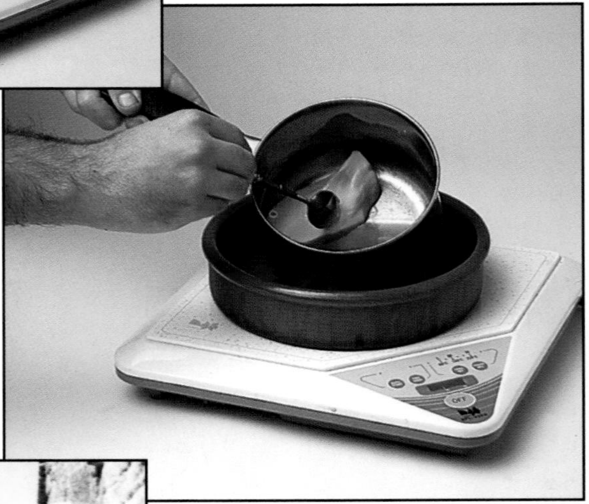

Fig.192. You will notice that in a very short time it will start to melt; once it is liquefied you can mix it with the colors.

193

Fig.193. The subject, as you can see, features interesting textures, and marked contrasts between light and shadows.

194

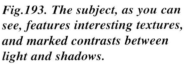

Fig.194. The sketch is made using a stick of carbon. There is no need to add much detail; simply draw in the elements of the composition.

First as normal, draw a sketch of the subject which will serve as a guideline for the elements to be included in the composition (fig.194 previous page).

When painting with encaustic it is best to leave aside the paintbrush, it is only used for details and finishing touches. To proceed, take the pigments with a spatula and mix them on the palette. When you have the color you want, add the liquid wax using the spoon that you used to stir it with. Stir the pigment and the wax with the spatula until they are properly mixed. Immediately apply the color on the surface of the support. I advise you to work swiftly as once the wax is removed from the heat it will solidify quickly (fig.195). Start by covering the wall on the left and the arch in the foreground, using layers of Raw Umber, Indian Red and Yellow Ochre with a touch of white. The darkest patches use the same colors with a little Ultramarine Blue and Crimson Madder (fig.196).

Continue working your way across the arch concentrating more on its form, the textural qualities of the stones, the shadows, the clefts and cracks between each block. With a mixture of Yellow Ochre and Cadmium Yellow, add the patches where the stones catch the light on the left of the arch, towards the center pick out some of the stones with a slightly orange umber color and along the top add some slightly darker colors, hints of blues and pinks. The darkest part, the underside of the arch, can be painted in Burnt Umber (fig.197).

Your next step is to apply an impasto in a uniform color which links the arch with the house on the right and, concentrating the top half of the picture, turn to the house in the middle ground and add a greenish patch with a fair amount of white (fig.198). You will notice that the main arch that is already painted is made up of a range of warm colors, while the house that is in the middle ground will be painted in a cooler range of colors.

195

Fig.195. The impasto gives the work a wide range of colors. It allows you to roughly mix colors that are coarse and unrefined.

Fig.196. You must work swiftly, when working with wax on a cold surface it solidifies rapidly.

196

Fig.197. The colors can be superimposed to obtain a greater effect of relief and to increase the color range. See how the volume of the arch is already clearly defined.

197

198

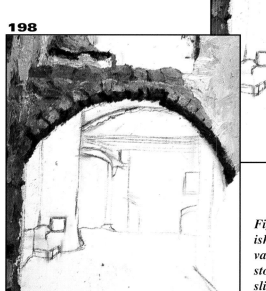

Fig.198. The arch is almost finished already. See the chromatic variations between the blocks of stone making up the arch, each a slightly different color dependent on its position and how the light catches it.

85

This is to contrast the two planes, setting them apart to avoid confusion. So, the arch in the middle ground is painted with a monochromatic range of greys (fig.199). With a medium paintbrush add in the doorway of the house on the left with an intense Ivory Black, with just a touch of thinner. The use of color in encaustic technique is of paramount importance as the medium doesn't allow detailed outlines but patches of color that are indistinct and undetailed. This is evident when you look at the steps of the house on the left or the finish on the stones which make up the arch in the foreground. Now focus on the ground, apply a grey mixed with a little Cerulean Blue and Carmine; try to avoid a uniform color and highlight the little variations in color, to suggest the irregularity of the paving stones. With Naples Yellow, paint the house at the end of the street with various gradations of color, the part closest to the door is somewhat darker. With a little Olive Green and Gall Green add in the deep shadow that the arch casts over the wall on the right (fig.200). The patch of sky is covered with a uniform white layer.

Now, with a medium brush use Cobalt Blue, Ultramarine Blue and a little Violet (thinned in turps so that the paint is almost a wash) to darken the paving stones, putting the street in the shade (fig.201). Once the paint has dried you will see how effective it is to add oils (fig 201). Take a fine brush and retouch certain cracks, surfaces and details on the doors, windows and walls which give further realism to the composition and increase its similarity to the original subject (fig.202).

199

Fig.200.The work has developed conside-rably,the white of the support has already been covered.Now retouch the colors by overlaying paint with a brush.

201

Fig.199.With just a few touches of encaustic you can capture the rugged and uneven textures of the stones.

200

Fig.201.By darkening the ground with a deeper blue tone,the street becomes more shady.
Fig.202.Retouch the door frames and other openings adding detail with a fine brush.Avoid overdoing it as you will lose other qualities of the work.

202

TIPS

If you want to make alterations to the picture once it has been finished,you can do so by using a heated metal palette knife on the area,to remove excess paint or to alter certain details.

If,once the work is finished,you decide to display it in your ·home,do not hang it above a radia-tor, in a warm place or in direct sunlight.

Drying time for encaustic is the same as that of oils,so avoid touching the surface of the picture with your fingers for at least a month and a half after it is finished.

203

With the same thin brush, add the plants on the wall of the house at the end with a little Permanent Green and Emerald Green and the plants growing along the top of the arch and the house with Emerald Green and touches of Indigo on the darkest parts.

Work with a free hand, agitated overlaid brushstrokes make the shapes and textures of the plant foliage more realistic.

As you can see, the finished work is impressive (fig.203). The qualities of this medium are evident to see. If you take a close look you will see that each layer contains a huge variety of colors which give the picture this finish characteristic of encaustic technique. The hardest task when painting with encaustic technique is to choose the right subject. You have to pick out subjects that offer a huge variety of textures (such as landscapes with plenty of rocks or dense woodland in the foreground). This technique is not suitable for all subjects. Be aware of its strengths and use this medium only when the subject choice will do it justice. Having reached this point, you may be tempted to continue adding details to give the picture a more photographic appearance. Don't make this mistake. You must appreciate the richness of this medium, don't undo all the work that you have put in, superimposing layers of color and creating varied textures in encaustic. Have another look at the original (fig.193) and compare the finished work (fig.203). You will see that the artist has concentrated his work on the surfaces of the walls, the ground and the rocks, leaving out the two figures who are running through the middle of the image. You should also learn to omit certain unnecessary elements; any details that are unsuitable for this medium, and to stress or even exaggerate textures and qualities of the surfaces that will work well with this particular wax technique.

Fig.203. The finished work speaks for itself. It is a work of pictorial skill. The task is, without doubt, a difficult one, but once you have learned to paint with wax, results such as this are not beyond your reach.

A Landscape in Fresco and Tempera

204

In this chapter I will be teaching you how to paint using fresco with finishing touches in tempera. This process requires you to prepare the support in advance and there are certain special conditions to take into account when painting. I advise that you pay careful attention to the instructions that follow for the correct use of this medium, you may even find it useful for decorating walls in your home or on any outside walls of your property.

Óscar Sanchís is once again going to be our guide, he will show us how this technique is developed; as well as the step by step painting exercise he will show us how to prepare the mural to paint on, using a wooden support as shown here.

Watch carefully, first we are going to describe how the mortar base is prepared. First, take a rigid support (a wooden board) which we will use to try out the technique (when you consider that you have had enough practice you can start painting on walls). I advise you to carry out tests first. On this support apply a mortar made of coarse sand and lime. While this layer is still damp, make a series of indents over the flat surface with a spatula so that the second layer will hold better (fig.204). When the first layer feels firmer and harder, spread another layer of mortar with a greater proportion of lime and finer sand. Apply this is the same way as the previous layer. (fig.205). Let this layer dry a little, but while it is still damp apply the final layer which contains a greater proportion of lime than the previous layers, mixed with crushed marble (fig.206).

205

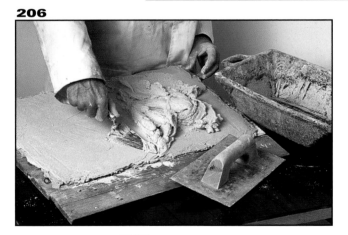

206

207

Fig.204. In order to practice fresco use a thick wooden board and apply the first layer of coarse sand mixed with lime.

Fig.205. Over this first layer apply a second, composed of finer sand and a higher proportion of lime.

Fig.206. Three coats are enough. The final one will be the painting surface and the mortar contains a higher proportion of lime as well as crushed marble.

Fig. 207. You must smooth out of the surface of the final layer so that it is flat and regular.

The final layer must be carefully smoothed as this is the surface onto which the fresco will be painted (fig.207 previous page).

Now you need to leave the mortar to settle. This will only take a couple of hours dependant on the humidity of the surroundings (if it is very humid it may take three to four hours). Before starting to paint, check that the surface of the mortar is still a little damp without being soft, i.e. it should be firm and hard without water sitting on the surface or retained water. Now you can start to paint. If you begin painting as soon as you have finished preparing the mortar, without letting it settle, all the colors will disappear, absorbed by the mortar which is too damp.

The subject that has been chosen is a beautiful rural view of Montrichard in the Loire region of France (fig.208). Start with simple subjects like this; when you have had more practice you will be ready to tackle more complex compositions.

You will be using powdered pigments diluted with water. Yes, simply water. You may be wondering "What about the binding agent?". The binding agent of fresco painting is the lime contained in the mortar, this is why the paint must be applied while the surface of the mortar is still damp.

Unlike the techniques discussed until now, the sketching is done without using a pencil or carbon stick. It is sufficient to paint with a monochrome wash - a sort of grisaille effect. It is best to paint with a light color, which can easily be covered by further washes of paint, fresco paints do not have effective covering power. As you can see, the artist has chosen a Yellow Ochre, as it appears consistently throughout the composition (fig.209).

It is important to begin with pale background colors as used here to represent the group of houses and the sky as the base color will have a resounding effect on the colors applied on top of it.

208

209

210

211

Fig.208. The subject is a little riverside community in the North of France, the image is a harmonious combination of blues and earth colors.
Fig.209. Primary pencil sketches are not used with fresco techniques. The subject is sketched with a single color in a similar way to a grisaille.

Fig.210. The sky is described using irregular washes, with a deeper blue dominating the top of the sky, growing paler as it reaches down to the horizon line.
Fig.211. After the first washes add the bridge in deep shadow and the trees on the hillside.

Large areas such as the sky are painted in one wash, with a color that has been prepared on the palette, because if you don't have enough prepared it is impossible to mix the same color again. As you can see, the sky has not been painted as a uniform plane, from the very start the shading has been introduced and built on to describe the position of the clouds. The sky at the top is darker and the color lightens as the sky nears the horizon (fig.210 previous page).

From here onwards you can work more freely, without worrying about colors and adding further contours with touches of color. The paint must be fluid but it shouldn't run. You can start strengthening the tones with Raw Sienna on the right side of the castle and Payne's Gray on the crowns of the trees. At the same time, you could apply dense washes to certain areas on the bridge using Burnt Umber and the same color mixed with Ultramarine Blue for the shadows (fig.211 previous page). Keep adding further washes which will help outline the structure of the bell tower, the castle walls, the roofs of the houses etc. With an intense mauve, paint the slate roofs and the windows of the bell tower; then concentrate on the river in the foreground painting it in Ultramarine Blue mixed with Dark Cadmium Yellow; use a little Cadmium Yellow and some Carmine to bring out the colors of the castle. The colors of the washes can be applied pure or mixed with a little lime, which lightens them and gives them better coverage (fig.212).

In this phase you can reinforce the tones, building the shapes with every brush stroke and creating contrasts between light and shadow. The shape and outline of the details can be retouched to give the image better definition and more contrast (fig 213). See how clearly the doors and windows of the houses on the river bank stand out.

Now we are ready to leave the fresco painting. In order to progress to the next step we have to leave the colors to dry for a few days.

When you return to the work you will

212

213

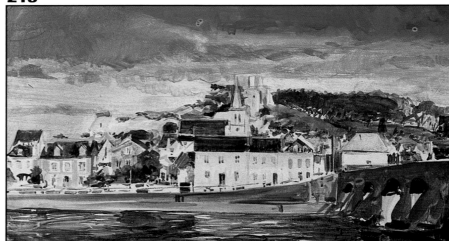

214

Fig.212. Paint the river in the foreground by overlaying horizontal irregular lines and add more details to the houses on the river front.
Fig.213. Paint the roofs of the houses, the doors and windows and the color of the facades. Work with fresco painting in washes just as you would use watercolors.
Fig.214. Compare this image with the one before and you will see how the colors appear lighter once the fresco has dried. You should bear this factor in mind when applying the paints.

see how the colors have lightened and the tones are different to when the mortar was still damp (fig.214 previous page). When the surface of the picture is dry it is time to apply the tempera, this medium always has to be applied onto a dry surface. Take the same pigments that you used when painting fresco and mix with egg yolk just as was explained previously under the heading "Painting with fresco and tempera".

As you will notice, once dry, fresco colors are more luminous than those of any other medium; the whiter the background the lighter the applied colors will appear. As tempera gives better coverage, it is used to emphasise the volume and make the shapes and contrasts stand out. You will notice how the artist has intensified the colors of the bridge, introduced more color to the facades of the houses and darkened the foliage of the trees.

Evidently, to paint these finishing touches in tempera (the pink clouds, the reflections of the roofs...) you should continue in the same manner, i.e. using veils of color or using more paint to create the play of light all over the surface of the composition. You can

paint over the fresco washes as tempera is more saturated. You have probably already noticed the limitations of this medium, the advantages or disadvantages (depending on your point of view) posed by the fact that your work has to conform to a strict time table which has been carefully planned beforehand and great care has to be taken when describing shapes and choosing colors. Artists not used to the medium tend to produce excessively pale paintings. If you want to avoid this mistake , simply paint with more intense colors than those you see in your model, in this way they will correct as they dry. If the tempera you apply starts to crack this could be because you hadn't left the layer of fresco beneath to dry for long enough. Try not to be impatient, don't ever paint with tempera onto a surface that is still damp. Bear in mind that tempera must always be applied onto a dry surface.

Fig.215. Fresco and tempera is one of the oldest and most established mixed media techniques, this doesn't prevent contemporary artists using it to great effect.

TIPS

- Note that there are some pigments that dissolve more easily in water than others. If you add a few drops of alcohol to the mixture it will help dissolve the pigment.
- When painting in fresco it is better to use paint brushes with long bristles; the best type is rounded at the tip. For very fine details you can also use brushes of fine hair.
- The colors should be stronger when you apply them, because when they dry the tones will fade.

Painting a Surrealist Composition

We are going to finish off this book with a creative step by step exercise, as well as giving you the opportunity to combine various techniques that have been explained earlier. This should set your imagination free. Óscar Sanchís is going to paint a Surrealist composition with traditional watercolors, anilines, *frottage* and *collage*. See how he does it and try repeating this exercise yourself.

First, make a drawing of an imaginary landscape full of strange objects and beings, like the example shown here. Take some paper, not too thick, a piece of A4 will do, and make frottages of materials that you have to hand with a colored pencil. Next, cut out pieces of this paper, cut them into shape and stick them to the paper (fig.216). Now paint the sky with anilines so that the wash fades in patches and paint the hills on the horizon with a wash of uniform gray (fig.217). With a medium sable paintbrush, paint the undulating bridge that appears in the center of the picture. Do this by mixing various colors which blend together with the *frottage* pattern lending the bridge a textured look (fig.218). Take up your traditional watercolors and paint the head of the snail that emerges to the right of the bridge. Use two colors initially, Raw Umber on the highlighted areas and Burnt Umber on the parts in shadow. Once the first wash has been added, develop the colors on wet, this will enrich the colors and create further contrasts and volume to the snail (fig.219). Next paint the steps, one by one with a Burnt Umber wash. Do the same with the tower on the left of the image using a violet wash (Cobalt Blue and Cadmium Red). The wall facing the right is shaded whereas the color on the other face is almost imperceptible (fig.220).

Work on the foreground using successive washes of Yellow Ochre, Sienna, Deep Cadmium Yellow and Burnt Umber. These colors should be painted on wet and in close progression so that the colors fuse. Look closely at how the artist has splattered some Prussian Blue aniline paint, he's created this effect by flicking the paint off the bristles of a toothbrush (as I explained in an earlier exercise).

216

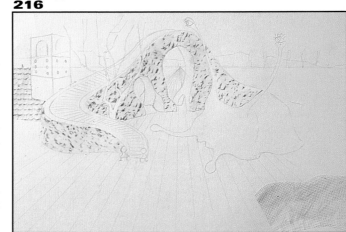

217

218

219

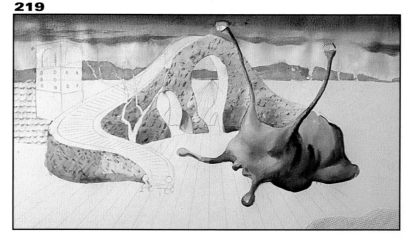

Fig.216. Having drawn the sketch of the model, make a collage by sticking on pieces of paper that have textured patterns obtained by rubbing a pencil over the paper pressed against various surfaces.

Fig.217. Paint the sky with anilines, leaving lighter patches for the clouds.

Fig.218. Paint the bizarre curved bridge in the center with a variety of colors. Paint on wet so that the colors merge with eachother.

Fig.219. Describe the disproportionately large head of the snail with just a couple of colors; the stronger the contrast between the colors the greater the sensation of volume created.

220

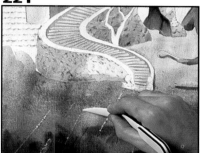

221

While the colors are still wet, scratch at the paper with a knife point to open white spaces on the picture's surface (fig.221).

Cover the middle ground with a blue wash and a very diluted gray on the plane that separates the foreground from the distant hills (fig.222). Load the paint brush with Burnt Umber and start to describe the bare trees in the middle ground (fig.223). As is normally the case, this last stage is for retouching, modifying colors, strengthening contrasts and harmonising the colors in the work. To achieve this, the artist has applied various washes in Gall Green on both sides of the central motif, he has darkened the brown washes in the foreground with Dark Cadmium Yellow. Here he has also added further detail to the composition, such as the eyes of the snail (using a fine brush), the line of distant trees, further retouches of color on the bridge and delicate washes on the head of the snail (fig.224).

222

I recommend exercises of this sort because, as well as heightening your imagination, it will allow you freedom from more commonplace themes which keep the artist slavishly focused on a model from which they draw all their references.

Fig. 220. With plenty of patience and a fine brush, paint each step.
Fig.221. Scraping with the point of a knife will open white spaces on the paper if it is still damp.
Fig.222. Painting alla prima with a large paintbrush, work on the foreground, overlaying Umber colors and Siennas, letting them spread and blend at random over the paper's surface.

223

Fig.223. With a fine paintbrush, retouch certain outlines and paint the group of trees with twisted bare branches in the middle ground.
Fig.224. The finished picture is a typical surrealist painting, one of the styles that is most capable of bringing together freedom of composition with boundless creativity and firm indifference to formal pictorial rules.

224

TIPS

- Don't base your subject on a photograph. Try to be creative, invent shapes and new settings. If you want, look at books on Magritte or Dalí's work to inspire you, although you should not try copying their paintings.
- If you are going to scratch the surface of the painting make sure that the paper is not too thin, so that you can do so without fear of damaging it.

Glossary

A

Acrylic. This paint has acrylic resin as a binder, which is made from a combination of chemicals or a derivant of petroleum.

Alla prima. A technique of painting, a direct résumé in one session, painting rapidly, without returning to retouch.

B

Binding agent. Substance that is mixed with the powdered pigment to make a pictorial medium.

C

Casein. A substance that comes from milk which, when mixed with pigments acts as a binding agent; it is often associated with tempera.

E

Enamel. Powdered glass which vitrifies on the surface.

Encaustic. A pictorial technique that consists of mixing pigments with hot wax which acts as a binding agent.

F

Fixer. An aerosol that is sprayed onto drawings made in carbon, chalks or pastels to stop the pigment from wearing off the picture surface.

Fresco. A pictorial technique for mural painting which consists of painting with pigments and water onto a coat of damp gesso.

G

Genre. A classification of the pictorial techniques such as sketch, landscape, figure study, interior etc.

Glaze. A coat of translucent color that is applied over another color in order to alter or intensify it.

Gum Arabic. Resin from the acacia plant which is used as a binder for watercolor and gouache.

I

Impasto. A technique that involves applying thick coats of color to create a textured surface.

L

Lacquer. Secretions obtained from a type of insect (today lacquer is made synthetically) which is used when making varnishes.

Lightfastness. The degree to which the pigments will discolor when exposed to the light.

M

Medium. The liquid in which the color pigment is suspended, for example linseed oil for oil paint or acrylic resin for acrylics.

Mixed media. A term used to describe the use of different paint media used in the same work or a combination of different supports on which the paint is applied.

Modelling. A sculpting term which can also be applied to drawing and painting to describe the way that shadows are introduced by the application of distinct tones of color, resulting in the creation of a three dimensional illusion.

Mural. Any pictorial process which is applied to a wall.

P

Paintbox. A metal, plastic or ceramic container used for keeping and mixing colors. When you open the box the indentations in the lid serve as a palette for mixing colors. Metal or ceramic containers are best for encaustic; wooden ones for oils and metal or plastic for watercolors and anilines.

Pigments. Powdered coloring agents which come from natural sources (although now they can be manufactured synthetically) which, when mixed with a binding agent form a paint.

Primer. A mixture consisting of Spanish White and glue size, which is applied to the support to obtain a suitable surface to paint on.

R

Reduction. The name given to the process of mixing a color with white.

Resin. A sap secretion from certain trees that is used to make varnish.

S

Saturation. The effectiveness of a color to obliterate other colors when using a mixture of colors or veils of color.

Sinopia. The underdrawing of a fresco.

Support. The surface used to paint or draw on, such as a wooden board, a canvas, a sheet of paper...

Sgraffito. A technique consisting of scraping the top of layer of color with a pointed implement to reveal the color of the layer beneath.

Sketch. The first stage of the work before you paint, a study, drawing or painting which describes the work definitively from the start. You can make many sketches before you succeed in developing the idea that you are attempting to express.

Solvents. Liquids used to dilute paints. The solvent for water based paint is water, for oily media it is turpentine, white spirits or sansodor.

Spanish White. Ground, washed chalk which is used for priming canvas and for white washes.

Style. In sculpture, drawing and painting it describes the manner of doing the work. This may be achieved in a brisk, agitated, delicate, slow or quick manner...The style of the artist defines him, it is the artist's own signature.

T

Tempera. Water based paint in which the pigment is mixed with glue extracts from animal or vegetable sources.

Texture. Recreation of a structural pattern on the picture's surface.

Transparency. A way of applying paint as a veil so that it allows the light or the previous wash show through.

Turpentine. A liquid solvent with comes from resin.

W

Wash. A way of painting that dates from the Renaissance. It consists of a work painted in a color diluted in water, generally sepia, although it can also be watercolor, Chinese Ink or anilines.

Wet, painting on. A technique which consists of painting on an area or wash that is wet either because water has just been applied or it has been recently painted, the artist will decide the degree of wetness dependent on the effect he is looking to achieve.

Acknowledgements

The author of this book would like to thank the following people and companies for their collaboration and support in the production of this volume of the Techniques and Exercises series.
Gabriel Martín Roig, for his work on the texts and the general co-ordination of the book; Antonio Oromí for his photographs; Vicenç Piera from Piera for his help and advice on drawing and painting equipment and materials; Manel Úbeda from Novasis for his help in production and photosetting and especially the following artists; Mª Ángeles Agesta, Bibiana Crespo, Jesoep Antoni Domingo, Manel Grau Carod, Ester Llaudet, Francesc Mas, Ginés Quiñonero and Óscar Sanchís for their illustrations and step by step exercises.